Opening up
James

ROGER ELLSWORTH

DayOne

Opening up
James
ROGER ELLSWORTH

The epistle of James is eminently practical and enduring in relevance. Roger Ellsworth has provided a worthy exposition that will facilitate thought-provoking interaction with this heart-probing letter.

Roger Ellsworth's pastoral insight into purpose, meaning and application of James will surely engender thoughtful gazing into the mirror of God's Word that roots out our bent toward empty religion and results in genuine blessing.

Bennie Tomberlin
Pastor, First Baptist Church, Fairfield, Illinois, USA

In a day when good exposition of God's Word is so rare, Roger Ellsworth's exposition of the book of James is a real gem. I recommend this book to my fellow-pastors who desire to rightly divide God's Word, as well as to all students of the Bible, for their continual edification and growth.

Patrick McGill
Pastor, Poplar Heights Baptist Church, Jackson, Tennessee, USA

*Dedicated to the good saints of
Parkview Baptist Church*

© Day One Publications 2009

First printed 2009

Unless otherwise indicated, Scripture quotations are from the New King James Version (NKJV)®. Copyright © 1982 by Thomas Nelson, Inc. Used by permission. All rights reserved.

ISBN 978-1-84625-165-8

British Library Cataloguing in Publication Data available
Published by Day One Publications
Ryelands Road, Leominster, England, HR6 8NZ
Telephone 01568 613 740   FAX 01568 611 473
email—sales@dayone.co.uk
web site—www.dayone.co.uk
North American e-mail—usasales@dayone.co.uk
North American web site—www.dayonebookstore.com

Printed by Gutenberg Press, Malta

Contents

List of Bible abbreviations

THE OLD TESTAMENT		1 Chr.	1 Chronicles	Dan.	Daniel
		2 Chr.	2 Chronicles	Hosea	Hosea
Gen.	Genesis	Ezra	Ezra	Joel	Joel
Exod.	Exodus	Neh.	Nehemiah	Amos	Amos
Lev.	Leviticus	Esth.	Esther	Obad.	Obadiah
Num.	Numbers	Job	Job	Jonah	Jonah
Deut.	Deuteronomy	Ps.	Psalms	Micah	Micah
Josh.	Joshua	Prov.	Proverbs	Nahum	Nahum
Judg.	Judges	Eccles.	Ecclesiastes	Hab.	Habakkuk
Ruth	Ruth	S.of S.	Song of Solomon	Zeph.	Zephaniah
1 Sam.	1 Samuel	Isa.	Isaiah	Hag.	Haggai
2 Sam.	2 Samuel	Jer.	Jeremiah	Zech.	Zechariah
1 Kings	1 Kings	Lam.	Lamentations	Mal.	Malachi
2 Kings	2 Kings	Ezek.	Ezekiel		

THE NEW TESTAMENT		Gal.	Galatians	Heb.	Hebrews
		Eph.	Ephesians	James	James
Matt.	Matthew	Phil.	Philippians	1 Peter	1 Peter
Mark	Mark	Col.	Colossians	2 Peter	2 Peter
Luke	Luke	1 Thes.	1 Thessalonians	1 John	1 John
John	John	2 Thes.	2 Thessalonians	2 John	2 John
Acts	Acts	1 Tim.	1 Timothy	3 John	3 John
Rom.	Romans	2 Tim.	2 Timothy	Jude	Jude
1 Cor.	1 Corinthians	Titus	Titus	Rev.	Revelation
2 Cor.	2 Corinthians	Philem.	Philemon		

Overview

The book of James was written by the half-brother of Jesus. During Jesus's public ministry, James did not accept him as the Messiah (John 7:5). His unbelief came to a screeching halt when Jesus appeared to him as the risen Lord (1 Cor. 15:7).

After his conversion, James ascended rapidly in the leadership among the early Christians, becoming the head of the Jerusalem church. In that position, he joined with the apostles Peter and Paul in helping the Jerusalem Christians understand that Jews and Gentiles would be saved in the very same way—through Christ alone (Acts 15:11). It is important to understand that James and the other leaders did not determine the way of salvation. They rather identified that which had been determined by God.

James also took the lead in developing a plan by which Gentile Christians could fellowship with their Jewish counterparts without giving needless offence (Acts 15:19–21).

The fact that the work of the Jerusalem Council, which probably occurred around AD 49, is not mentioned in James's letter probably indicates that the letter was written prior to it, perhaps as early as AD 44. This would make it the earliest of all the New Testament books.

The letter shows that James had a pastor's heart. He wrote from Jerusalem to Jewish believers who had been scattered by persecution. It is most likely that this was the persecution instigated by Herod Agrippa I (Acts 12).

Known as 'James the Just' because of his righteous living, James encountered persecution himself, being put to death in AD 62, according to the historian Josephus.

10

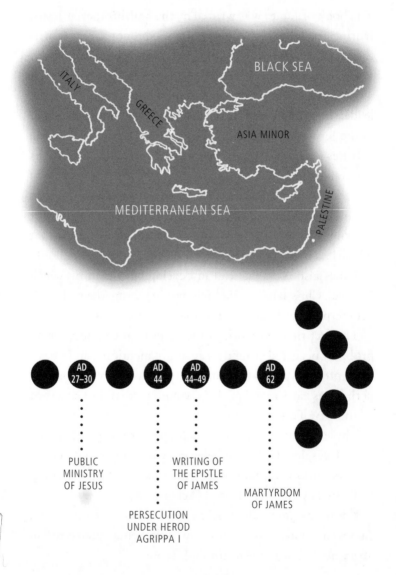

BLACK SEA

ITALY

GREECE

ASIA MINOR

PALESTINE

MEDITERRANEAN SEA

AD 27–30

AD 44

AD 44–49

AD 62

PUBLIC
MINISTRY
OF JESUS

WRITING OF
THE EPISTLE
OF JAMES

MARTYRDOM
OF JAMES

PERSECUTION
UNDER HEROD
AGRIPPA I

Background and summary

Four men in the New Testament were named James. There was the James whose son Judas was one of the twelve disciples (Luke 6:16). There was James the Less, that is, James son of Alphaeus, who was one of the twelve. Then there was the James with whom we are best acquainted—son of Zebedee, brother of the apostle John, and one of the three disciples who were closest to Jesus. Finally, there was James the half-brother of Jesus, who would become the leader of the Jerusalem church (Acts 15).

The reason why we refer to him as the half-brother of Jesus should be obvious. While he and Jesus had the same mother, they did not have the same father. Jesus had no earthly father, having been conceived in Mary by the Holy Spirit of God (Matt. 1:20). This James is the one who wrote the epistle that bears his name.

But why should we study this epistle? The answer is because James deals with several issues that challenge believers in Christ. Here are a few:

- the challenge of suffering (1:2–4)
- the challenge of 'the gap' between hearing and doing (1:21–27)
- the challenge of not playing favourites (2:1–13)
- the challenge of maintaining good works (2:14–26)
- the challenge of controlling the tongue (3:1–12)
- the challenge of resisting the world (4:1–10)
- the challenge of sickness (5:13–18).

We surely cannot look at this list without realizing that the book of James is a book for us.

We can think of it in other terms. The key verses of James are these: 'If anyone among you thinks he is religious, and does not bridle his tongue but deceives his own heart, this one's religion is useless. Pure and undefiled religion before God and the Father is this: to visit orphans and widows in their trouble, and to keep oneself unspotted from the world' (1:26–27).

On the basis of those verses, we can say that James wrote to warn his readers about the danger of useless religion. We are trying to determine why we should give ourselves to a study of James, and here is a question that will help us: Is there any useless religion around? Or we can put it another way: Do we see any evidences of people merely going through the motions of religion? Do we see any signs of people professing faith in Christ without any evidence of it showing up in their lives? Do we see any evidences of the apostle Paul's warning that some have a form of godliness while denying its power (2 Tim. 3:5)?

If so, we have our answer. We need the epistle of James. It will help us attack stale, humdrum, useless religion, and will move us to reality in religion.

With that in place, let's turn our attention to two things: how James began his letter, and what he emphasized in his letter.

How James began

In the first verse of the letter he identifies himself as 'a bondservant of God and of the Lord Jesus Christ'. We might say he began with the consciousness of what he was and what he owed.

What he was

James realized what he was. Who was he? A servant! He understood that he existed solely for the purpose of carrying out the desires of another: God himself. James understood that God did not exist to serve him, but rather he to serve God.

It sounds like a terrible thing to be a servant, but it is not a terrible thing to be a servant of God. Life's greatest meaning and its greatest joy lie in this kind of servanthood.

Is it going too far to suggest that we have in James's identification of himself a clue to finding reality in religion? Some never experience such reality because they insist on coming at it from the wrong end. Try to turn Christianity on its head by making it a matter of God serving you instead of you serving God, and the power and joy of it will elude you. But turn it right side up by understanding that you are to serve God and that you will never have a higher privilege than being nothing but a servant, and you will no longer have to look for joy in Christianity. The joy of it will find you.

What he owed

James realized what he owed. Where do we find this truth? It is right there in those words 'the Lord Jesus Christ'.

The word 'Lord' means 'exalted one'. It is the name of divine sovereignty. 'Jesus' is a human name. And 'Christ' means 'anointed one'. It refers to one being set apart to perform certain tasks. Put them together and you have a world of truth. The Lord of glory took our humanity so he could perform for us the work of salvation. More specifically, he took our humanity so he could be our prophet, priest and king. As our prophet, he declares the truth of God to us. As our priest, he offered himself as the sacrifice for our sins. As our king, he rules over us to the glory of his dear name.

It concerns some that James only mentions the Lord Jesus twice in this epistle: in his opening verse and in the opening verse of chapter 2. But look at how he refers to Christ in his second reference: 'our Lord Jesus Christ, the Lord of glory'. It was not necessary for him repeatedly to mention the name of Christ to prove that his heart was filled with love for Christ.

So James began his letter, as the old hymn says, 'Near the Cross'. That is, by the way, always a good place to begin, a good place to stay and a good place to end. We will never have to look far for reality in religion if we are near the cross.

That brings us to consider our second point.

What James emphasized

A quick tour of this epistle finds James putting the spotlight on certain things.

The Word of God

How James loved God's Word! It is God's saving word (1:18, 21), 'the perfect law of liberty' (1:25) and 'the royal law' (2:8).

No Christian will ever grow beyond an affection and esteem for the holy Word of God.

Prayer

James gets to this matter very quickly (1:5), returns to it (4:2–3) and ends with it (5:13–18). It was obviously much on his mind. We shouldn't be surprised at this; James himself reportedly spent much time in prayer. Eusebius, church historian of the fourth century, quotes Hegisippus regarding James: 'He used to enter alone into the temple and be found kneeling and praying for forgiveness of the people, so that his knees grew hard like a camel's because of his constant worship of God.'[1]

Good works

James did not believe, as is often assumed, that we are saved by our works. He was one with the apostle Paul in affirming that we are saved by faith and faith alone. But while he did not believe in salvation by works, he most definitely believed in a salvation that works. In other words, he would have none of this teaching that suggests that we can be saved and have no interest at all in serving the Lord. And this is exactly what Paul himself taught (Eph. 2:10). One of the good works with which James was most concerned was caring for the needy (1:27).

Finally, we can say that James also emphasizes:

Separation from the world

To put it another way, James teaches that Christians should not allow the world to dictate what they think and how they behave.

The world is the enemy of God and, therefore, of the Christian. No one can be a friend of God and a friend of the world (4:1–5).

There are other emphases in this letter as well, but surely no one can doubt that the ones I have mentioned are in the category of major emphases. And just as James's identification of himself gave us a clue to finding reality in religion, so do these major emphases. Do we want to find true power and joy in religion? Let us look to these matters: Scripture, prayer, good works and separation from the world. That is a good and challenging agenda!

1 Comfort in suffering

(1:1–4)

There can be little doubt that this book was written by James the half-brother of Jesus (230 words of this letter closely resemble the words of James in his message at the Jerusalem Council—Acts 15:13–21). The book of James is considered to be the earliest of all the New Testament epistles. It was probably written some time between AD 45 and 50.

James wrote to Jewish Christians who were 'scattered abroad'. The book of Acts tells us that the Christians in Jerusalem were compelled by persecution to scatter throughout Judea and Samaria (Acts 8:1) and even as far as Phoenicia, Cyprus and Antioch (Acts 11:19). Fleeing did not always solve the problem, as many Christians also encountered persecution in their new homes.

The trials of life often shake our faith and cause us to let up in service. In other words, hardships and difficulties can diminish the reality of religion. James wrote to help his readers have such reality.

The Bible has quite a bit to say about Christians suffering. It tells us about the suffering of some of its greatest heroes. Job, Moses, Joseph, Paul and Peter are just a few who had to endure exceedingly difficult circumstances.

Persecution

A good part of what the Bible calls 'suffering' comes under the heading of persecution. This is the hardship and pain inflicted on Christians by those who are opposed to their message. This form of suffering was so prevalent in the early church that many Christians gave up their lives for their faith. It was such a common threat that many of the New Testament writers found it necessary to warn their readers to be prepared for it. The apostle Peter, for example, made persecution the dominant theme of his first epistle.

We may think this form of suffering is relegated to those long-ago days, but it isn't. Many Christians are even now suffering severe persecution in various places around the world, and hostility towards Christians is increasing in many nations.

Life-circumstances suffering

But persecution is not the only kind of suffering Christians must endure. There is also what we might call 'life-circumstances' suffering. No one is persecuting us, but there are all kinds of circumstances that make life very difficult and challenging.

Most of us think of this type of thing when we hear the

word 'suffering'. This was the type of suffering Job had to endure.

It's interesting to note how James introduces the matter of suffering. He says, 'My brethren, count it all joy when you fall into various trials ...' (v. 2). There is no 'if' there. It was not a matter of whether or not trials were going to befall his readers, but of when the trials would come. Trials in this life are inevitable for the Christian (Phil. 1:29; 1 Thes. 3:3). The key question in the mind of the Christian is not, then, whether trials will come, but rather how to deal with them when they do come.

It was not the purpose of James to give us a full-blown theology of suffering. He makes only a brief mention of it before moving on. But by ranging over the Scriptures in general, we can find certain guidelines and principles to help us cope with the trials that befall and beset us.

A distinction

First of all, Scripture would have us distinguish between suffering that we bring upon ourselves and suffering that the Lord brings upon us.

> Scripture would have us distinguish between suffering that we bring upon ourselves and suffering that the Lord brings upon us.

The apostle Peter made this distinction when he addressed the matter of persecution. He told his readers to make sure that the persecution that came their way was undeserved (1 Peter 4:15–16).

The same distinction may be applied to the type of suffering we are concerned with. The law of sowing and reaping is still in effect. Our choices lead to consequences. If we make good choices, we can expect good consequences; but if we make evil choices, we can expect evil consequences.

If we abuse our bodies, our health will deteriorate and we may very well put ourselves in an early grave. If we abuse those around us, our relationships are going to deteriorate. If we fail to feed and nurture ourselves spiritually, our walk with God is going to deteriorate.

We all know these things are true, but when the consequences of evil choices begin to pour in, we are ever inclined to ignore the law of sowing and reaping and lament our circumstances by crying out, 'Why is God doing this to me?' But in this situation God is only letting us experience the consequences of what we ourselves have chosen.

The proper response to this type of suffering is to break with that pattern of behaviour that has brought the suffering upon us.

Suffering from God's hand

But let's go to that form of suffering that most troubles Christians, that suffering that comes, so far as we can tell, apart from us making evil choices. How do we handle this type of suffering?

The crucial thing is to remember that such suffering comes from God's hand. Nothing is clearer in Scripture than the truth that God sends trials and difficulties into the lives of his children because he has certain purposes to achieve.

Take the suffering of Joseph, for example. It came upon him in wave after wave. His hateful brothers sold him into slavery. He ended up in Egypt, where he was framed for something he did not do and was cast into prison. And it all came upon him through no real fault of his own. Joseph must have spent a good bit of his time wondering why all these things befell him. Years later, he had his answer. He was able to see that God had a purpose in it all. It was so that he, Joseph, could be the means of saving his people from terrible famine. Joseph put it in these words: 'But as for you, you meant evil against me; but God meant it for good, in order to bring it about as it is this day, to save many people alive' (Gen. 50:20).

Other Scriptures also give testimony to God's purposes in sending suffering. The psalmist writes, 'Before I was afflicted I went astray, but now I keep Your word' (Ps. 119:67). Yes, God sometimes sends suffering to chastise us for our sins and make us more scrupulous about obeying his commands (Heb. 12:5–11).

Sometimes God's purpose in sending suffering is to make our faith strong and to make us more Christlike. One aspect of Christlikeness is patience, a virtue James specifically says is produced by trials.

Sometimes God's purpose in sending suffering is so his people may demonstrate their faith in him. We may rest assured that unbelievers are always watching how we react to the difficulties of life. They formulate their views of Christianity from what they see or do not see in us. If they see us continuing to trust and serve the Lord in the midst of our suffering, they will be convinced that there is something to our faith. If they see us respond to our suffering by becoming hard and bitter towards God, they will feel justified in concluding that there is nothing to our faith.

God's purpose in sending suffering is always to bring glory to himself. The apostle Peter says faith that is 'tested by fire' will at last be found to bring 'praise, honor, and glory' to Christ (1 Peter 1:7). In this life, we aren't always able to see how our suffering can possibly bring honour to God. But it isn't necessary for us to see it in order for it to be true.

> In this life, we aren't always able to see how our suffering can possibly bring honour to God. But it isn't necessary for us to see it in order for it to be true.

How does God get glory in our suffering? Over here is a Christian who has suffered terrible illness for a long time, and he says he would not have been able to bear it if God had not been with him to strengthen and help him. That brings glory to God.

Over there is a Christian who has suffered financial hardship, and she talks about how the promises of God have encouraged and comforted her through it all. When God's faithfulness to his promises is emphasized, God is glorified.

The end of suffering

All of this brings us to a final truth. We can find strength to face suffering by looking to that unspeakably glorious time when all our sufferings will finally be over.

Yes, such a time is coming! The Bible assures us that it is true. The tears of this life will be wiped away. Sorrow will dissolve. Death itself will be finally and for ever crushed.

The Bible constantly warns us not to become so intoxicated with this life that we fail to look beyond it to the life to come. That forward look has the marvellous ability to transform the suffering of this present time. As we dwell on the glory to be revealed we shall most certainly find ourselves saying with the apostle Paul, 'For I consider that the sufferings of this present time are not worthy to be compared with the glory which shall be revealed in us' (Rom. 8:18).

And let us never forget how it is that we have confidence regarding the life to come. It is through no merit of our own, but solely because of the redeeming work of our Lord Jesus Christ there on Calvary's cross.

James urged his readers to 'count it all joy' when they fell into 'various trials'. He wasn't suggesting that they greet every difficulty that came their way by exclaiming, 'Whoopee! Isn't this wonderful?'

No, not at all. Christians are not to pretend that the sufferings of this life are not real and painful. They are rather to find joy in the midst of their suffering, and they do so when they can say it has not come because of sinful choices, when they trust the Father's loving purpose in it, and when they can look beyond it to see that coming day when all suffering will be over.

FOR FURTHER STUDY

1. Read 1 Peter 4:12–19. What does the apostle say about how we should respond to suffering?

2. Read 2 Corinthians 4:16–18. Why do Christians not need to lose heart in their suffering?

TO THINK ABOUT AND DISCUSS

1. Many Christians are being persecuted for their faith. What can you do to help?

2. What times of suffering have you experienced? What are some of the things you have learned from these times?

2 Wisdom in trials

(1:5–8)

As we have noted, James was writing to believers who were in the midst of great suffering. Much of this suffering was in the form of persecution. These people, having come to faith in Christ, were being ostracized and attacked.

J ames's first words about their suffering may very well have taken them by surprise. He told them to 'count it all joy' that they were facing these circumstances.

How could he say such a thing? It was because of his firm conviction that their suffering was not meaningless. It was, rather, God's way of bringing them to spiritual maturity.

Suffering is still the subject when we come to the verses of our passage. As we examine these verses, we can see James making three points: trials demand wisdom, wisdom demands prayer, and prayer demands faith.

Trials demand wisdom (v. 5)

It is legitimate to ask God for wisdom in each and every circumstance of life. How often we find ourselves lacking it! But we never need wisdom more urgently than when we are facing difficulties.

First, a word about wisdom. What is it? We must not confuse it with knowledge. Knowledge is information; wisdom is application. Knowledge is comprehending facts; wisdom is handling life. Knowledge is theoretical; wisdom is practical.

We can think of it in terms of driving a car. We can have very good knowledge of a car and not drive very well at all! Conversely, we can have little knowledge of how a car operates and still expertly handle it.

Life is a lot like driving a car. We are tooling along, and suddenly someone darts out in front of us, or a huge pothole appears. In those situations, we must know how to respond in such a way that we are able to preserve our lives and the lives of others.

The trials and difficulties of life are much like the driver who pulls in front of us or the potholes in the road. We are driving along the roadway of life, and suddenly a trial comes. We need wisdom to respond to that trial. We need to know how to respond in such a way that we do not encourage a mistaken notion about what Christianity is. We need to know how to respond in such a way that we do not dishonour God. We need to respond in such a way that we do not discourage our fellow-Christians.

How often Christians drive the car of faith into the ditch when a trial pops up in the road!

Wisdom demands prayer (v. 5)

But how do we find wisdom for the facing of trials? James provides the answer: 'If any of you lacks wisdom, let him ask of God …'

'If any of you lacks wisdom …'! That includes all of us! No one is sufficient in and of himself to face the trials of life, but the Lord is sufficient for his people.

We are once again face to face with the importance of prayer. How much the Bible makes of it! And how very poor we are at practising it!

> Prayer is such a wonderful resource. It connects our poor, feeble little lives with the almighty God.

Prayer is such a wonderful resource. It connects our poor, feeble little lives with the almighty God. It constructs a pipeline from his sufficiency to our inadequacy.

I do not doubt for a moment that most of us pray when we face trials. The question James puts before us has to do with that for which we are praying.

We pray for the trial to be lifted, and there is nothing wrong with that. But has it occurred to us to pray for wisdom in the trial? Have we asked God to help us handle it in such a way that we bring glory to him and leave a positive impression on those around us?

James attaches a glorious promise to his plea for prayer. He says that God 'gives to all liberally and without reproach'

(v. 5). To say that God gives 'liberally' is to say that God is generous. He is not a miserly God who delights in withholding blessings from his people. John Calvin says the Lord is ready 'to add new blessings to former ones, without any end or limitation'.[1] Someone has suggested that we should think of God's liberality in giving in terms of a pitcher always tilted and ready to pour. God's pitcher of blessing is always tilted to fill the cups of his people.

That phrase 'without reproach' means that God gives without finding fault. One of the great things about God is that he knows of what we are made. He knows we are mere dust. He knows how very weak we are. He knows how difficult life is for us. He understands why we struggle so. He does not find fault with us for being what we are.

King David put it wonderfully:

As a father pities his children,
So the LORD pities those who fear Him.
For He knows our frame;
He remembers that we are dust.

(Ps. 103:13–14)

So let us be about the business of praying! We often vex ourselves with the matter of why our prayers are not answered. James would have us understand that the unanswered prayer is not our main problem in praying. It is rather the unasked prayer (4:2)!

Prayer demands faith (vv. 6–8)

After telling his readers to ask God for wisdom, James impresses upon them the importance of doing so in faith.

To ask in faith is to ask without doubting. James proceeds

to liken the doubting person to one who is 'like a wave of the sea driven and tossed by the wind' (v. 6). The picture James draws is of a cork bobbing in the waves, carried first towards the shore, then away from it.

James adds to this picture by calling such a person 'double-minded' (v. 8). This is the man who is struggling with two minds. One mind tells him to trust God, but he no sooner resolves to do so than the other mind begins to point him to all his problems and suggests that they are too great even for God! So back and forth he goes between God and the problems—like the bobbing cork!

We must, then, pray in faith! But here we come to a point of much confusion. What does it mean to pray in faith? Most people I encounter have a mistaken notion of faith. They think it means that we pick something out that we want God to do, and then we psych ourselves up to believe that he will actually do it. Faith to these people is exactly the same thing as positive thinking.

And with this definition in place, many are disappointed and angry with God. They wanted God to do something, they asked him for it and they were really convinced that he would do it. And it didn't happen! Many are in this boat! And now they are saying, 'This faith business doesn't work. I know: I tried it. I asked God, I believed and nothing happened.'

The problem is not with God. Rather it is with a mistaken understanding of faith. Faith is not believing that God will do what we want done. Rather it is believing that God will do what he has promised to do.

In this passage, James gives us a distinct promise. He tells his readers that God will give them wisdom for the handling of their trials if they will ask him in faith. In other words, if they will believe, and not doubt, God's promise to give them wisdom, they will receive that wisdom when they ask for it.

Many fail in the asking part. Others ask but do not believe. We must both ask and believe! And God will grant the wisdom. That is the promise.

We may not feel as if we are getting the wisdom. We usually don't feel it while we are in the situation, but as time passes and we look back on the situation, we will be able to see that God did indeed give us the wisdom for which we asked.

It is not our business to determine whether God is actually giving us the wisdom for which we ask. It is our business to do the asking and to leave it with God to do as he has promised.

From the shores of eternity, we will finally be able to see all clearly. When we do, we will see that God answered more of our prayers than we thought at the time, and we will see that he gave us more wisdom in those times than we realized.

For further study ▶

FOR FURTHER STUDY

1. Read Matthew 7:7–12. What does the Lord Jesus teach about prayer in this passage?
2. Read Romans 10:17. What is the basis of faith?

TO THINK ABOUT AND DISCUSS

1. In what way can you illustrate the difference between wisdom and knowledge?
2. What can you do to improve your prayer life?

3 The high low, the low high and the high high

(1:9–12)

In these verses, James continues to encourage his readers. Many of them were facing tremendous pressures. They were finding that their faith in Jesus was making life very difficult for them. As Jews, they were disliked by many Gentiles, and as Christian Jews, they were disliked by many of their fellow-Jews.

James offers encouragement in these verses by making use of what we know as a 'paradox'. A paradox is a statement that is true even though it seems to contradict common sense. G. K. Chesterton defined a paradox as 'truth standing on its head shouting for attention'.[1] In response to that definition, Kent Hughes wrote, 'In my mind's eye I see truths lined up like ridiculous people on their heads, feet waving in the air, calling: "Hey, look at me! Up is down! Down is up! Think about it."'[2]

As James thinks about his readers, it occurs to him that the persecution many of them are facing could, in fact, have a divisive effect upon their fellowship as believers. He seeks to avoid such division by using the paradoxes of the 'high low' and the 'low high'. He then adds a word about that which we can call 'the high high'.

The high low (v. 9)

In this verse, James addresses himself to 'the lowly brother'.

Whom did he have in mind? There is no difficulty here. He was addressing all of his readers who were poverty stricken as a result of the persecution they were encountering. Kent Hughes writes of these: '… because they were economically low, they were low in the eyes of the world and, no doubt, in most instances low in their own eyes. Their poverty produced a lowliness of mind.'[3]

James did not want the terrible circumstances of these people to make them think of themselves as second-rate or inferior Christians. To keep this from happening, he encouraged them to take pride in their high position.

And what was their high position? It is right there in that word 'brother'. Their poverty could not negate or nullify that word. No matter how low they were in terms of the world's goods, they were exceedingly rich in spiritual terms. They had been plucked from the condemnation and ruin of sin by the saving work of Jesus Christ and had been made part of the family of God.

We need this word quite as much as James's readers. This is a day in which many Christians are being made to feel inferior because of their faith. These days, we are frequently told that we are guilty of hate crimes if we adhere to the teaching of the Bible. Here is an example. The Bible teaches us that Jesus Christ alone is the way to heaven. But as we embrace that and share it with others, we find ourselves accused of being intolerant!

Many Christians find themselves constantly beaten down at work or in school or, perhaps, even among friends and family. And, while it may not be so much the case in the West, it is certainly true that many Christians in other places are actually suffering from poverty because of persecution.

Every Christian who feels life's cruel pounding can crawl into the warm wisdom offered by James. No matter how detested we are in this world, no matter how low and despicable we appear to be, we actually enjoy the highest of all privileges, namely, being part of the family of God.

James's point in verse 9 can be stated, then, in this way: The key for the low Christians is to keep in mind their high position in Christ.

> No matter how detested we are in this world, no matter how low and despicable we appear to be, we actually enjoy the highest of all privileges, namely, being part of the family of God.

The low high (vv. 10–11)

But not all James's readers were being persecuted. Some were doing quite well. Their property had not been seized. They had not been refused the right to do business and to make money. In some way or another, either they had managed to avoid detection, or those who had detected their Christianity had chosen to be tolerant.

The temptation facing these Christians, whom James

classifies as 'rich', was to think that they were better off than their suffering brothers because they were better in some way.

We still have the tendency to equate prosperity with God's blessing and adversity with God's displeasure. But James would have none of this. He wanted the rich Christians not to shun those in their midst who were worse off than themselves, but rather to embrace them as brothers and sisters and treat them as equals.

> James calls for rich Christians to stay humble by remembering that the riches of this life are fleeting and unpredictable.

If the key for the low Christians is to remember their high position in Christ, the key for the high Christians is to remember their low position as mortals. In other words, James calls for rich Christians to stay humble by remembering that the riches of this life are fleeting and unpredictable. Life in this world passes very quickly. It is like withering grass and the fading flower. And when we get out into eternity, we will not be rich Christians and poor Christians. We will all be the same in heaven.

We must be careful we do not misunderstand what the Bible says about riches. It is not against God's people being rich. Abraham was rich. Job was rich. David was rich. It is rather against Christians allowing their riches to make them proud, elitist and presumptuous.

Those Christians who are not rich should never envy or mistreat those who are. It is possible for a Christian in poverty to be just as much a snob as a Christian in prosperity.

The high high (v. 12)

Having encouraged low believers to think of their high position in Christ and high Christians to think of their low position as mere mortals, James moves to a point that unifies and thrills Christians of all stations in life. He writes of 'the crown of life which the Lord has promised to those who love Him' (v. 12).

The crown of life! What does it mean? James was obviously drawing on something with which all his readers were familiar, namely, the realm of sports. Here are some runners preparing for a race. They strip off everything that would weigh them down and step up to the starting line. Every muscle is taut and every nerve ready as they await the signal. And they're off! Each puts every ounce of strength and energy into the race, straining for the finish line. What does the winner receive? He or she is crowned with the victor's wreath.

Through this imagery James was affirming that Christians are running a race that will end in glory. That is where the finish line is!

But there is a difference. All Christians are winners as they cross that finish line. There the Lord God himself will greet them and will crown their efforts with eternal life.

And in glory there will be no rich Christians and no poor Christians. There will simply be believers in Jesus who are astonished and amazed that the God of glory was gracious enough to forgive them their sins.

The key for us in this life is to keep our eyes trained on the finish line in glory. How very easy it is for us to get our eyes on the wrong things! How very easy it is for us to look with disfavour on fellow-Christians because they are lower than we are, or because they are higher!

If we keep our eyes fixed on eternity, these lesser matters will be seen as lesser matters. In eternal glory, God's people will experience the 'high high'. They will be as high as they can possibly go, and nothing will ever be able to bring them down.

So let us keep eternity in mind even to the point that we daily repeat the prayer of Joseph Bayly: 'Lord, burn eternity into my eyeballs!'

FOR FURTHER STUDY

1. Read Ephesians 1:3–14. What blessings exalt the poor Christian to a high status?
2. Read Psalm 49:16–20. In what way does this passage help the rich Christian?

TO THINK ABOUT AND DISCUSS

1. What can rich Christians do to help their poor brothers and sisters?
2. What can poor Christians do to help themselves?

4 From trials to temptations

(1:13–18)

James's readers were living in tough times. They were Jewish Christians who were being persecuted for their faith.

Persecution posed many problems for these early Christians. One of those problems may be somewhat surprising to us. Persecution constituted for many a temptation to sin! In what way? First, many Christians were strongly inclined to reply in kind: 'If they hurt me, I will hurt back!' We might call this the 'don't get mad; get even' temptation.

But temptation sprang from persecution in another way, namely, the inclination to use persecution as a justification for sin. In other words, some of those who were suffering for their Christianity were reasoning along these lines: 'My life is so difficult that I am entitled to do whatever I can to make it more pleasurable.'

People have often allowed their difficulties to give them a sense of entitlement. Some of them have even allowed themselves to conclude that God is the source of their temptations. They may very well have reasoned along these lines:

- God has sent the trial.
- The trial has caused me to be tempted.
- Therefore, God has tempted me to sin.

This has been going on since Adam and Eve sinned in the Garden of Eden. Adam blamed Eve, and Eve blamed the serpent. But notice that, in blaming Eve, Adam stressed that it was God who had given her to him (Gen. 3:12). The whole fiasco was God's fault! Someone has said, 'To err is human; to blame it on the divine is even more human.' This type of thing led Will Rogers to say that there are two eras in American history—the passing of the buffalo and the passing of the buck!

So in these verses, James moves from trials to temptations. In doing so, he clears God of wrong-doing and indicts the true culprit.

God is cleared (v. 13)

James is very plain and emphatic: 'Let no one say when he is tempted, "I am tempted by God …"' His reason is equally clear: 'God cannot be tempted by evil …' This means, as one writer puts it, God is 'untemptable'.[1]

God cannot tempt anyone to sin because he cannot! His very nature is so opposed to sin that he cannot possibly tempt anyone in that direction. D. Edmond Hiebert writes, 'God is unsusceptible to evil; evil has never had any appeal for Him. It is repugnant and abhorrent to Him.'[2]

But if God does not tempt anyone to do evil, why did Jesus teach us to pray, 'do not lead us into temptation' (Matt. 6:13;

Luke 11:4)? The answer, of course, is that here the word 'temptation' does not mean temptation to sin. It rather refers to trials. It is a fact that the Lord does regularly send trials to his people so they may know their spiritual condition. Asking God not to lead us into temptation means, then, that we ask him not to test us because we are already aware of how very weak we are.

The true culprit is indicted (vv. 14–15)

If God cannot tempt us to evil, how is it that we sin? James answers, '… each one is tempted when he is drawn away by his own desires and enticed' (v. 14). He leaves no doubt about it. We are individually responsible for sin. We sin because we are sinners.

But is not Satan the culprit? Do we not sin because he tempts us to sin? Indeed he does! And James is not denying that. But the truth of the matter is that Satan could not have any success with us at all if it were not for the stuff of which we are made.

Satan has to have something to work with in order to lead us into sin, and our nature gives him plenty to work with! We do not possess the nature of God which gives us a complete abhorrence for sin. We rather possess a nature that readily inclines us towards it. Just as the hog has a nature that inclines it to wallow in the mud, so we have a nature that inclines us to sin.

How did we get this nature? The Bible leaves no doubt about this. It tells us that we were all present in Adam when he sinned. His sin was our sin (Rom. 5:12)! And the result of that sin is that we are all fallen creatures. We are no longer as God made us. We originally had a desire for God, but sin killed off that desire and replaced it with a desire for sin!

James uses two vivid images to convey to us how sin does its work.

Fishing

The first image is drawn from fishing. Curtis Vaughan observes, 'The words translated "drawn away" (lured) and "enticed" (ensnared) are taken from the language of fishing.'[3] R. V. G. Tasker notes that the imagery is that of '... a fish swimming in a straight course and then drawn off toward something that seems attractive, only to discover that the bait has a deadly hook in it'.[4]

Childbirth

The second image is drawn from childbirth. Vaughan says, 'The suggestion is that man's lust, like a harlot, entices and seduces him. Man surrenders his will to lust, conception takes place, and lust gives birth to sin.'[5] Andrew Ross notes, 'The mere fact of our being tempted does not involve in and of itself anything sinful. It is when the desire of man goes out to meet and embrace the forbidden thing and an unholy marriage takes place between these two, that sin is born.'[6] Kent Hughes expands this picture:

> There are two births here. First, evil desire gives birth to sin. And second, sin gives birth to death ... The idea is that sin grows rapidly, just as an embryo grows to maturity, and when it is full-grown, the state of pregnancy must end. But the horror here is, sin does not give birth to life, as would normally be expected, but to death.[7]

So both images end in death. The fish takes the bait, is hooked and pulled to shore, where it dies. The childbirth results in death.

The point is unmistakable. Sin is not the light, casual thing which we make it out to be. It always leads to death. Gordon Keddie is correct: 'You can only be a fun-loving sinner for so long. Soon the bill has to be paid.'[8] And the final instalment of the death to which sin leads is eternal death, which means nothing less than separation from God, and all that is good, for ever.

> We can respond by ignoring the sombre reality of divine judgement, but pretending that it is not true will not make it go away.

No one likes the thought of God's eternal wrath, but the Bible is unrelenting in its declaration of this reality. It is a truth written large in Scripture, and the Lord Jesus himself was the foremost proclaimer of it.

We can respond by ignoring the sombre reality of divine judgement, but pretending that it is not true will not make it go away. Or we can respond by accepting the teaching of the Bible and by embracing the way of escape it presents.

Hope is presented (vv. 16–18)

The path on which James has led us would be sorrowful indeed if there were nothing more to be said. If we could talk only about sin and death, we would be most miserable. But James refuses to leave us in unrelieved gloom. There is something that breaks the power of sin and delivers us from spiritual and eternal death. It is nothing more than the power of God working in the human mind and heart to grant spiritual life (v. 18). As that spiritual power works in us, we are made into new creatures.

Having spiritual life and being new creatures doesn't mean we are beyond the possibility of sin. That is still to come in eternal glory! But it means that the grip of sin is broken to the point that it no longer dominates our lives.

How does this spiritual life become ours? We most certainly cannot produce it ourselves. We can no more will ourselves into spiritual life than we can will our way into physical life. Granting spiritual life is God's work!

But God graciously does this work! And there lies our hope! If you even now find yourself tired of the grip of sin and longing for new life, it is indisputable evidence that God is working in you. So flee to him! Thank him for the evidences of his working and plead with him to work more! Ask him to make your sin very real to you, and ask him to make his salvation even more real to you.

And what about us if we are Christians and find ourselves struggling with temptation? The answer lies in us recognizing that we have already received spiritual life, and in nurturing that life. As James will soon point out, that nurturing can only take place as we give careful attention to the Word of God (v. 21).

For further study ▶

FOR FURTHER STUDY

1. Read Genesis 3:1–6. How did Satan tempt Adam and Eve to sin?

2. Read Matthew 4:1–11. How were the temptations of Jesus similar to that faced by Adam and Eve? How did Jesus triumph over these temptations?

TO THINK ABOUT AND DISCUSS

1. What temptations are you facing at the moment? Name some steps you can take to ward off temptation.

2. What can we as Christians do to increase our awareness of the enormity of sin?

5 The goodness of God

(1:16–18)

In his wonderful commentary on the book of James, Kent Hughes writes, 'It is impossible to walk with God if we question his goodness.'[1] But believers can do this very thing. We can attempt to walk with God while we question his goodness.

It was so with James's readers. As we have been noting, they were suffering severe persecution because of their faith in Christ. This persecution was causing many of them to be disappointed in and angry with God. A good God would not allow such things to happen to his people!

Doubt of God's goodness is as old as the human race. Masquerading as a serpent, Satan came to the Garden of Eden and approached Eve: 'Has God indeed said, "You shall not eat of every tree of the garden?"' (Gen. 3:1). He was casting doubt on the goodness of God. 'Is it really true that God does not allow you to eat of all the trees of the garden?' The implication, of course, was that if God were truly good, he would have allowed Adam and Eve to eat of all the trees without so much as a single exception.

Satan has never let up on this business of questioning the goodness of God. Sickness comes, a loved one dies, friends fail, conflict comes; and Satan sidles up to say, 'If God were really good, you wouldn't be going through this.'

Satan also works the other side of the equation. In other words, he not only uses the presence of difficulty but also the absence of some blessing: 'If God were really good, you would have this thing or that.'

James may very well have had Satan's deception of Eve in mind when he addressed his readers: 'Do not be deceived, my beloved brethren' (v. 16). He essentially says, 'You must not let Satan deceive you about the goodness of God as he deceived Eve so long ago.' Any time we doubt the goodness of God, we are falling prey to Satan's wiles. We are deceived!

With that in place, James offers three resounding affirmations about the goodness of God.

God is the only source of goodness (v. 17)

Look at what James has to say: 'Every good gift and every perfect gift is from above, and comes down from the Father of lights …' He seems to be calling his readers to conduct something of an inventory. It is as if he were saying, 'Look around you. What do you call "good"? Make no mistake about it. If you call anything "good", it comes from God.'

The same truth applies to us. What do we call 'good'? Good health? Family? Firm and unfailing friendship? Freedom? The smile of a child? The singing of the birds? The thunderous crash of the waves? The majesty of the mountains? The warmth of a fire in the winter and the cool of the breeze in the summer? These all come from God—and thousands of other things, too!

If it is good, it comes from God! That is James's assertion! And if it comes from God, there is no good that comes from any source other than God!

It was this realization that led Asaph to say to the Lord, 'Whom have I in heaven but You? And there is none upon earth that I desire besides You' (Ps. 73:25).

God is the unchanging source of goodness (v. 17)

James adds a glorious dimension to our understanding of God's goodness by saying that there is 'no variation or shadow of turning' with 'the Father of lights'.

James is stressing for us the constancy, or faithfulness, of God. In calling God 'the Father of lights', he is taking to the realm of astronomy. This is a realm of constant variation. Stars vary in brilliance. The moon waxes and wanes. The sun rises and sets. It creates all kinds of shadows and sometimes is eclipsed.

> God does not have days when he has more goodness than on other days. His goodness is always undiminished and unchanged.

But that which is so commonplace in the realm of astronomy is never true of God. With him there is never any waxing or waning or any kind of eclipse. He is always the same. And that means he is always good.

God does not have days when he has more goodness than

on other days. His goodness is always undiminished and unchanged. Kent Hughes says, 'God does not change like shifting shadows. God's goodness is always at high noon.'[2] The devil will tell you otherwise. He will tell you that God has less favour towards you today than he had for you yesterday. And it is your fault!

But listen to James: God is good. He always has been and he always will be. He cannot be anything other than good. And this means that God is being good to us even when our circumstances seem to be shrieking that he is not good.

God is the source of the supreme act of goodness (v. 18)

James has affirmed that the Lord is the source of goodness and that his goodness will never change or fail. If he had said nothing more, we could go our way with our hearts singing!

But James has more to say! In verse 18, he calls our attention to the supreme act of God's goodness, namely, his granting spiritual life to his people.

> God's gift of spiritual life must be called his supreme gift because it rescues us from the supreme tragedy.

Why is it appropriate to call this the supreme act of God's goodness? The answer is not hard to find. We come into this world in a state of spiritual death (Eph. 2:1–4), and spiritual death finally empties into eternal death, that is, eternal separation from God.

God's gift of spiritual life must be called his supreme gift because it rescues us from the supreme tragedy. It is no wonder that the apostle Paul exclaimed, 'Thanks be to God for His indescribable gift!' (2 Cor. 9:15).

What does James tell us about this supreme expression of God's goodness? The first thing is that it is the result of God's initiative, or God's grace. James says, 'Of His own will He brought us forth …' Just as we could not will ourselves into physical life, so we cannot will ourselves into spiritual life. Matthew Henry says of salvation, 'The original of this good work is here declared: it is of God's own will; not by our skill or power; not from any good foreseen in us, or done by us, but purely from the good-will and grace of God.'[3] Kent Hughes adds, 'We are God's people because of a total act of grace rooted in God's unprompted goodness.'[4]

But how does God channel his saving grace to us? James has the answer. He says it is 'by the word of truth' (v. 18). It is through the preaching of the Word of God that our minds are enlightened. The Word of God shows us our sinful condition and the wrath to come. But, thank God, it also shows us that the Lord Jesus Christ did everything necessary for our sins to be forgiven and for us to have a right standing with God.

The apostle Paul refers to the Word of God as 'the sword of the Spirit' (Eph. 6:17). It is the instrument that the Spirit of God uses in bringing us to spiritual life.

The source of salvation is the grace of God. The channel is the Word of God. And the outcome is 'that we might be a kind of firstfruits of His creatures' (v. 18).

The term 'firstfruits' refers to 'the choicest part' or 'the pick' of humanity. This was James's way of showing his readers the supreme honour of their position.[5] The Puritan Thomas

Manton put it in his own quaint way. He said of believers and God, 'The world are his goods, but you his treasure.'[6]

So let us hear the conclusion of the whole matter: God is good! There is no goodness apart from him. There is no changing in his goodness. And there is no getting around the fact that salvation is his greatest goodness.

Don't let anyone ever tell you otherwise. God is good!

FOR FURTHER STUDY

1. Read Psalm 107. How many times does your translation use the word 'good' or 'goodness' in reference to God? What manifestations of God's goodness do you find in this psalm?

2. Read Ephesians 2:1–10. What expressions of God's goodness does Paul cite? Why is it accurate to call this the 'supreme goodness'?

TO THINK ABOUT AND DISCUSS

1. Write down some of the ways in which God has expressed goodness to you.

2. How do you explain difficult circumstances as expressions of God's goodness?

6 Appropriating the Word of God

(1:19–21)

We must keep reminding ourselves that James wrote his letter to Christians who were experiencing terrible persecution. This created all kinds of problems for them, and James wrote to give them guidance and encouragement.

One of the problems created by the persecution was the tendency to doubt the goodness of God. It was the 'If God is good, why is this happening to me?' syndrome.

James responded to that problem by affirming three things about the goodness of God: he is the only source of goodness, he is the unchanging source of goodness and he is the source of the supreme act of goodness. The supreme act of goodness is, of course, the goodness of salvation, and that goodness flows to those who believe through the Word of God.

His mention of the role of the Word of God in salvation took James to yet another problem associated with his readers' persecution, namely, how they could find strength to face it.

Can we relate to these people? The problems of life demand strength, and we often feel that we have no strength. The demands are great and reserves are depleted! The question of James's readers is, then, the same that we often find ourselves asking: Where can we find strength for the living of these days and the facing of our difficulties?

James's answer is plain and emphatic: strength is found in the Word of God! Every Christian has already experienced the strength of God's Word. Salvation is nothing less than a demonstration of the power of God's Word. Each believer was once in the spiritual graveyard—dead in trespasses and sins!—but the Word of God came and brought spiritual life. God used the truth of his Word to save us.

Now that same powerful Word is still available to us. God did not use his Word merely to save us and then withdraw it. No! It is still available, and it is still powerful. If we want strength for living, then, we must look to the Word of God.

But as powerful as the Word of God is, it will not infuse its strength into us if we do not appropriate it. And it is this business of appropriation that James addresses in the verses before us.

What must we do to appropriate the Word of God? We can summarize what James says in three words: swiftness, filthiness and meekness. Proper appropriation of the Word means developing swiftness, laying aside filthiness and cultivating meekness.

Developing swiftness (v. 19)

James urges his readers to be 'swift to hear'. And swiftness in hearing means being 'slow to speak, slow to wrath' (v. 19).

Be swift to hear! The Word of God is more necessary to us than our food. It is more precious than gold. It is a lamp unto our feet and a light unto our path. We cannot live properly without the Word of God!

How very eager we should be to read it and hear it taught! Nothing, absolutely nothing, should be more important to us than taking it in!

But our age will not go down in history as 'the age of hearing'. Adlai Stevenson once opened an address to students at Princeton with these words: 'I understand I am here to speak and you are here to listen. Let's hope we both finish at the same time.'[1] But the truth is, a lot of church attenders get through listening long before the pastor gets through preaching.

Part of it is due to the short attention span created by the media. Another part of it is that we are largely lazy and undisciplined. Yet another part of it is that we are constantly encouraged on every hand to talk. The thinking seems to be that if we talk enough, we will come to discover important truths. But the greatest part of it is that we do not prize the Word of God as we should.

Be slow to speak! The worship services of those days often featured people interrupting the speaker to share their own 'insights'. And sometimes those 'insights' were 'outsights'—out of touch with reality!

But there is another way in which we need to be slow to

speak, namely, to ourselves. In other words, when the Word of God is being declared, we must be on guard against the tendency to be inwardly raising objections.

Be slow to anger! When the Word of God is accurately preached, we will often find that it hurts. It is a sword that pierces and cuts (Heb. 4:12)! How do we respond when this happens? Do we become resentful and combative? If we allow anger to come in, the Word of God will not come in!

> When the Word of God is accurately preached, we will often find that it hurts. It is a sword that pierces and cuts (Heb. 4:12)!

Some fail to appropriate the Word of God because they are angry at the one who is delivering it! Perhaps they have seen a flaw in him. Or perhaps they disagree with something he has done in leading the church. Those in this category would do well to heed James's word about being slow to anger.

What searching words James has given us! These are days in which the tendency is to be slow to hear, swift to speak and swift to anger!

Laying aside filthiness (v. 21)

James says, '... lay aside all filthiness and overflow of wickedness'. The word 'filthiness' means all that defiles us in God's sight. The Puritan Thomas Manton said the word was sometimes used for the filthiness of ulcers and for the nastiness of the body when sweating.[2]

The word 'overflow' does not mean that some wickedness is all right and the Christian should only be concerned about excess in wickedness. James's point is that we are to get rid of remaining sin. Curtis Vaughan writes, 'The thought then is that sin, though renounced by Christians, is not entirely vanquished in them. There may be some wickedness remaining, like a bad "hangover" from pre-conversion days, as one commentator puts it.'[3]

Cultivating meekness (v. 21)

James urges his readers to 'receive with meekness the implanted word, which is able to save your souls'. What does it mean to receive the Word of God?

James uses the Greek word *dechomai*, which means 'a welcoming or appropriating reception'. It's the same word Luke used to describe the Bereans' response to God's Word: '… they received the word with all readiness, and searched the Scriptures daily to find out whether these things were so' (Acts 17:11). Paul also used the same word to describe the response of the Thessalonians who, when they heard God's Word, 'welcomed it not as the word of men, but as it is in truth, the word of God' (1 Thes. 2:13).

So what does receiving the Word of God mean? James says, 'receive with meekness the implanted word.'

The word 'meekness' tells us that we are to come to the Word with a soft, gentle, teachable disposition, recognizing the authority of God's Word and submitting to it.

But what does James mean by the phrase 'the implanted word'?

The Word of God has already been implanted in each and every Christian. How is it possible, then, to 'receive' a word which is already implanted? John Calvin suggests that

James is saying we are to receive the Word so 'it may be really implanted'. In other words, we are to go on receiving the Word of God in such a way that it becomes more firmly and deeply planted in our lives than ever before. We are to go on opening our hearts to it and welcoming it so that its truth will be transfused and transmitted into our lives.

Here are some closing thoughts on this matter of hearing the Word of God:

- Both hearers and proclaimers of the Word carry a heavy responsibility for the success of the preaching of God's Word.
- Receiving the Word of God requires us to prepare ourselves in advance. We must think about what the Word of God is and how very blessed we are to have it.
- When it is time to hear the Word of God, every believer would do well to silently say, 'Speak, Lord, for your servant is listening' (see 1 Sam. 3:10).

For further study ▶

FOR FURTHER STUDY

1. Read Psalm 119. What are some of the things that the Word of God does for us? What can we do to show that we value the Word of God?
2. Read Hebrews 5:11. What problem does this verse identify?

TO THINK ABOUT AND DISCUSS

1. In what ways does the Bible strengthen you?
2. What advice can you give to a fellow-believer who expresses the desire to prize the Word of God more?

7 Applying the Word of God

(1:22–25)

James's readers were looking for strength to face their trials, and James was able to tell them where to find it. It was in the Word of God! The strong Word that had saved them (v. 18) was still available to them.

B ut availability was not enough. The Word of God would not infuse its strength into their lives apart from their own diligent efforts. First, they had to be diligent about taking the Word in (vv. 19–21). And then, as our text so clearly declares, they had to be diligent in applying it.

Listening to the Word of God is important. We must always begin there. Many church members fail in the listening. Let us be forever clear on this: we cannot possibly succeed in the Christian life apart from the regular intake of the Word of God. We can go further. Refusal to do this indicates that we have no spiritual life in us!

But while we must always begin with hearing the Word

of God, we must not stop there. We must apply what we have heard. James writes, 'But be doers of the word, and not hearers only, deceiving yourselves' (v. 22). His meaning is quite plain. Just as the person who has no interest in hearing the Word of God is horribly deceived about his or her spiritual condition, so is the person who is content to hear and not obey.

> No Christian obeys perfectly. But every Christian has a desire to obey God, is making efforts to do so and is grieved by failure.

No Christian obeys perfectly (1 John 1:8). But every Christian has a desire to obey God, is making efforts to do so and is grieved by failure.

To drive home the importance of this matter of obedience, James likens the Word of God to a mirror. Anyone who has any familiarity with Scripture knows that James is correct. It is indeed like a mirror! We cannot look into it very long without seeing ourselves for what we are!

But there are different ways to look in a mirror, and this is what James emphasizes in the verses of our text.

The forgetful glancer (vv. 23–24)

We all know that lots of things can go wrong with our faces! And we depend on mirrors to tell us what is wrong. A man does not want to go out in public with blood on his collar from shaving. And a woman doesn't want to be seen with lipstick on the end of her nose.

So we look in the mirror. But what would you think about a person who looks, sees a problem and then fails to correct it? You would say that there was absolutely no point in that person looking in the mirror. Looking in the mirror only works if it leads to action. Otherwise, it is useless.

With this in mind, we must say that there is a lot of useless looking in our churches. The Word of God, like the mirror, does its work. We look into it, and it tells us the truth about ourselves. And then the responsibility rests squarely on us! Are we going to correct the problems, or are we going to ignore them? Are we going to act on the Word, or are we merely going to walk away?

What does the Word of God reveal to you when you look into it? Does it tell you that your prayer life is not what it ought to be? What are you going to do? Are you going to begin to pray as you should? Does it tell you that you have bitterness and resentment towards a brother or sister in Christ? What are you going to do? Does it tell you that you are not as diligent as you should be about your study of it? Does it tell you that you are not as faithful in attending worship as you should be? Does it tell you that your love for Christ has grown cold?

How do you respond? Are you going to go on as you have been? Or are you going to take action?

This, by the way, is what the Word of God commands us to do! Take action! Many seem to be waiting for something to happen to them—some great spiritual experience!—that will make them do what they ought to do. Meanwhile, the Bible tells us to take responsibility for ourselves. It tells us not to wait for a feeling, but rather to begin to deal with those things that it has revealed.

There is no more urgent business before us than

addressing those matters in our lives which the Word of God has called to our attention. But how many refuse to do so! They are like the witch doctor who saw herself in a mirror owned by a missionary. The figure before her was so hideous that she jumped back from it. Immediately she began to bargain with the missionary for the mirror. Realizing that she would not take 'no' for an answer, the missionary finally agreed to a deal for the mirror. No sooner was the transaction complete than the woman grabbed the mirror and dashed it to the ground. When the missionary asked why she did this, the woman replied, 'It won't be making ugly faces at me any more!'[1]

The Bible reveals our ugliness to us, but the ugliness does not go away by us ignoring the Bible. It only goes away as we take the proper measures.

We can be thankful that James included another option.

The thoughtful gazer (v. 25)

This is the person who 'looks' into the Word of God and 'continues' in it.

The word 'looks' comes from a Greek word which suggests far more than a casual glance. Curtis Vaughan says it 'has the sense of looking carefully, closely, or seriously into a thing'.[2] He adds, 'It speaks of stooping down so as to see an object more clearly or to know it better. The word is used in John 20:5 of the beloved disciple stooping and looking into the empty tomb. Thus the word seems to denote a minute, searching inspection.'[3] And such careful scrutiny is not occasional but habitual. James says the thoughtful gazer into the Word 'continues in it'.

What is the purpose of this ongoing, penetrating gaze? It is to master God's Word with a view to putting it into practice.

Isn't it interesting that James here refers to God's Word as 'the perfect law of liberty'? God's Word is a 'law' because it was given by God for the express purpose of guiding and regulating conduct. It is 'perfect' because it was given by God himself. God who is perfect cannot produce anything that is not perfect. It is the law of 'liberty' because it gives liberty to those who subject themselves to it.

Satan works very hard to portray sin as the greatest freedom and God's Word as the greatest bondage, but just the reverse is true. Thomas Manton says, 'Duty is the greatest liberty, and sin the greatest bondage.'[4]

James's use of this phrase for God's Word ought to make us realize how very blessed we are to have it! A mirror to show us the truth about ourselves! The law that gives us liberty! If we could only realize to a fuller degree what we possess in God's Word, we would find ourselves struggling less to be thoughtful gazers!

We cannot leave James's words about this matter without noting the promise that he attaches to looking carefully into God's Word. The one who does so 'will be blessed in what he does' (v. 25).

We are accustomed to defining the word 'blessed' as 'happy'. But it is better to define it as 'fulfilled'. People are constantly striving for peace and fulfilment. These are restless days! And in their quest for fulfilment, people try pleasures and possessions. Some seek it in their careers. Some even seek it in drink and drugs.

But the more we seek fulfilment, the more it eludes us.

Where, oh where, can it be found? James says it is found in doing the Word of God. We should not be surprised at this. We were made by God and for God. Doesn't it make sense, then, that we can only find fulfilment in God?

If you want to be blessed, be a doer of the Word. Put James to the test! Live according to the Word of God, and see if James was not telling the truth about the matter.

FOR FURTHER STUDY

1. James likens the Word of God to a 'mirror'. Go through Psalm 119 again. What figures or pictures does it use for God's Word?

2. Read Hebrews 4:12. What picture does it employ for the Word of God? What pictures do we find in Jeremiah 23:29?

TO THINK ABOUT AND DISCUSS

1. How would you respond to a person who says that the Bible is too restrictive?

2. In what ways have you found the Bible to be a mirror?

8 Three marks of true faith

(1:26–27)

James has been emphasizing the Word of God. His readers were in need of strength to face the persecution that was coming their way. And that strength was available in God's Word. It had already manifested its strength in their salvation, and it was ready and able to manifest its strength again.

But they needed to appropriate it and apply it. In other words, they needed to devote themselves to taking it in and living it out. A strong Word is of no avail if we do not avail ourselves of it.

The verses of our text deal with this matter of living out the Word of God. James here identifies three things that are essential parts of living out the Word of God: taming the tongue, caring for the needy and avoiding worldliness.

We must note that he does not regard these as optional matters. We cannot ignore these things and still regard ourselves as having truly come to Christ. Our religion is 'useless' if it does not tame our tongues, move our hearts and separate us from the world. Anyone who thinks otherwise 'deceives his own heart' (v. 26).

The fact is that James considers these practices to be so very important that he devotes the rest of his letter to developing them. He takes up caring for the needy in chapter 2. He goes into detail about controlling the tongue in the first twelve verses of chapter 3. And from verse 13 of chapter 3 to verse 6 of chapter 5, he elaborates on separation from the world.

As we look at each of these, we must examine ourselves.

Taming the tongue (v. 26)

James first calls his readers to 'bridle' their tongues.

The word 'bridle' tells us how James regarded the tongue. It is like a powerful, rearing horse, which can take us on a wild ride if we do not hold the reins tight. Kent Hughes says, 'If you've ever sat on 1,500 pounds of restless bone and muscle and then hung on at full gallop, you have the idea.'[1] James was saying to each of his readers, 'You have a horse in your mouth!'

When do our tongues gallop like out-of-control horses? They do so when we gossip, which someone has defined as 'the art of confessing others' sins'. Our tongues gallop when we use them to express profanity and blasphemy. They also gallop when we use them to lie.

It could very well be that they gallop most often in the form of complaining and criticizing. How very easy it is for us to fall into this trap! Someone sings, and we find fault. Someone preaches, and we find fault. Someone teaches a class, and we find fault.

All of these and more are evidences of an unbridled tongue, and habitual practice of such things indicates a heart that is not right with God. The tongue reveals what is in the heart! The Lord Jesus himself said, 'Either make the tree good and its fruit good, or else make the tree bad and its fruit bad; for a tree is known by its fruit. Brood of vipers! How can you, being evil, speak good things? For out of the abundance of the heart the mouth speaks' (Matt. 12:33–34).

I want to emphasize that which I have already stated, namely, that James is talking about what is habitually true of us. Every child of God speaks inappropriately from time to time. James and Jesus are not talking about that which is occasionally true of us, but rather that which is continually true of us. Let the word go out loud and clear: continuing in sin is evidence that we have never been saved!

The great Methodist preacher John Wesley was once confronted by a very critical woman who said, 'Mr Wesley, the strings on your bow tie are much too long.'

Wesley secured a pair of scissors and asked the woman to trim them to her liking. After she did so, Wesley said, 'Your tongue, madam, is an offence to me—it's too long! Please stick it out … I'd like to take some off.'[2]

We would all do well to take this to heart and determine that we are going to take the scissors of repentance and do some trimming! How much good could we accomplish if we were to do so? How many of our children would have a different attitude towards the things of God if they could see that our religion brings us joy instead of making us crabby? How many of our friends would be convinced of the reality of our faith if our mouths were full of praise instead of profanity?

Caring for the needy (v. 27)

James tells his readers to visit the orphans and the widows in their trouble. These two groups of people were the most helpless in that time. So James was calling for his readers to show compassion to the most helpless.

There is something here that we must not allow to slip by. James was writing to people who had troubles of their own! And yet he tells them that they must not forget to show compassion to others! One of the very best things we can do for ourselves when we are in trouble is to help someone else who is in trouble.

> One of the very best things we can do for ourselves when we are in trouble is to help someone else who is in trouble.

There are all kinds of aching, hurting people around us, and we must not simply turn our heads and pass by.

One of the saddest dimensions of our day is that so many Christians are so absorbed with their seminars, charts, notebooks, study groups and discipling techniques that they don't have the time to bake a pie, send a card or mow the grass for the sick, the elderly and the lonely. It's easy to be a very good Pharisee while the world cries for a good Samaritan.

By the way, James is not alone in making this emphasis. We can find it in several other Scriptures, one of which is from the apostle John:

But whoever has this world's goods, and sees his brother in

need, and shuts up his heart from him, how does the love of God abide in him? My little children, let us not love in word or in tongue, but in deed and in truth. And by this we know that we are of the truth, and shall assure our hearts before Him.

(1 John 3:17–19)

Separated from the world (v. 27)

James calls his readers to keep themselves 'unspotted from the world'. The word 'unspotted' can also be translated 'unsoiled' or 'unpolluted'.

To be unstained from the world is to maintain both personal integrity and moral purity. It's to refuse to allow the world to set the standards for our beliefs and our conduct.

This is a polluting world! It can pollute our thinking, our speaking and our doing. Many who profess to be Christians give evidence of that pollution. They have set aside the clear teachings of the Word of God because they do not want to be out of step with what the world says. The authority for these people is not the Bible. It is the latest opinion poll!

And many who profess Christ have been polluted in their speaking. They talk just like everyone else. They would rather run the risk of offending God than sound different!

And many who suppose themselves to be Christians have polluted behaviour. They order their lives in exactly the same way as those who make no profession of faith at all.

There was a time when Christians considered it to be essential to be different from the world. They believed that only by showing the difference could they hope to attract unbelievers. Now, in a crazy flip-flop, the church is often saying the opposite. The church is trying to attract the world by being just like the world, not realizing that if Christianity is not different, there is no need for it! We can't hope to influence the world for Christ if we allow it to influence us in our thoughts, words and deeds.

As we have noted, we shall find James developing later in this letter his points about controlling the tongue and caring for the needy. The same is true on this matter of being separated from the world. Here is one of his most telling and biting statements about the world: 'Do you not know that friendship with the world is enmity with God? Whoever therefore wants to be a friend of the world makes himself an enemy of God' (4:4).

So James has set quite an agenda before us. Controlling the tongue! Caring for the needy! Staying separate from the world!

Is it possible to be saved and fail in these areas? Sure. But it is not possible to always be failing in these areas and be saved! May God help all of us to search our own hearts.

For further study ▶

FOR FURTHER STUDY

1. Read Ephesians 4:29–5:7. What does Paul teach here about Christian speech?
2. Read John 17:14–17. What does Jesus say about the Christian's relationship to the world?

TO THINK ABOUT AND DISCUSS

1. Are there people you know (or know of) who are in need? What can you do to help them?
2. What can you identify in your speaking, thinking or acting that indicates that you are too much influenced by the world?

9 Two visitors in church

(2:1–7)

James's readers were looking for strength to face the persecution that was coming their way, and James has been telling them that this strength is available in the Word of God. More specifically, he has been urging them to both take it in and live it out. And he has not left them in doubt about what is involved in living out the Word of God. It will involve taming the tongue, caring for the needy and maintaining separation from the world.

We might say that James has been putting general principles in place. Now he turns his attention to working out the details. He has listed caring for the needy as one of the marks of true faith. He now devotes all of chapter 2 to this matter.

What must we do if we are to practise such care? One thing we cannot do is ignore those in need! And this is exactly what we do when we show favouritism to those who are well-to-do.

We have to hand it to James—he certainly knew how to get attention and make his point. He did so through creating a hypothetical situation.

His readers have come together for their church service. On this particular day, there are two visitors. The first is obviously a very rich man. James calls him a 'gold-fingered' man in gleaming apparel. The other man is nothing like this at all. He is dressed in shabby clothes that are both grimy and tattered. Imagine it! Mr Gold Finger and Mr Grimy in the same church on the same day!

But the people of the church take scant notice of the second man because they are so enamoured with the first. They want to make sure that he is made to feel welcome. Just think of what he could do to advance the church if he were to join! They make sure he has the best seat in the house! And the poor man? Any place is good enough for him! It is embarrassing that he should decide to show up on the very same day as the rich visitor!

There is certainly nothing wrong with a man being rich or with making him welcome in church. The problem lies in treating him differently from the poor man. In so doing, the members of the church are acting as judges with 'evil thoughts' (v. 4). They are acting on the basis of wrong standards.

It should also be noted that James is not calling upon his readers to be impolite. We do not commit the sin of favouritism if we ask a teenager to stand or to sit on the floor so an elderly person can have a comfortable seat.

Why is showing partiality wrong? We can lift out of James's discussion two major reasons.

The poor are often rich in the very thing that Christians prize most (vv. 1, 5).

What is that thing which Christians prize? James makes this point at the very beginning of this section. It is 'the faith of our Lord Jesus Christ, the Lord of glory' (v. 1).

Some fuss with James because he only names the Lord Jesus twice in this letter (1:1; 2:1). But the issue is not the number of times James mentions Jesus, but rather the way in which he mentions him. There is in 2:1 a depth of feeling and spirit of worship that tell us all we need to know. James truly gave Jesus pre-eminence.

Why do Christians so value and esteem the Lord Jesus? It is all here in James's words.

- We prize Jesus because he is Lord—the sovereign, exalted ruler of the universe.
- We prize Jesus because he is Jesus. This is his human name. Wonder of wonders! The sovereign Lord took our humanity and dwelt among us.
- We prize Jesus because he is Christ. This name refers to his office or function. It means 'anointed one', and the Lord Jesus was anointed by God to discharge a threefold office—prophet, priest and king. As prophet, he faithfully declares the truth of God. As priest, he offered himself as the sacrifice for sinners. As king, he rules over his people.
- We prize Jesus because he is the Lord of glory. He is the Lord from glory who perfectly reflects the glory

of God and will eventually take his people to share in his glory.

- We prize Jesus because we, by the grace of God, 'hold the faith of our Lord Jesus Christ'. Faith is the means God gives by which we apprehend or appropriate who Christ is and what he has done. We know Christ by faith.

These things make it easy for each Christian to identify with the Roman emperor Theodosius, who said he would rather be a Christian clown than a pagan emperor![1]

Every Christian prizes Christ, but the Christian who is poor in the things of this world often prizes him more. James asks, 'Has God not chosen the poor of this world to be rich in faith …?'

> Poor people are generally richer in faith. Why? Because, since they have no other wealth, they prize more the wealth they have in Christ.

Let us not misunderstand what James is saying. A person is not automatically saved because he or she is poor materially. All who are saved—poor or rich—are saved by the grace of God through faith in Christ. But God has generally saved more poor people than rich (Luke 18:24–25; 1 Cor. 1:26–29). And poor people are generally richer in faith. Why? Because, since they have no other wealth, they prize more the wealth they have in Christ.

So James argues that favouritism is wrong because it belittles the very one they should prize, the one who is most likely to prize his or her faith.

Now he comes to his next argument.

The rich are often very poor in an area of great Christian need (vv. 6–7)

The believers of that day needed the same thing that they have needed in every era—the freedom to proclaim and practise their faith without fear of reprisal. But the Christians of James's day were being deprived of this fundamental right, and the rich were the ones who were doing the depriving! They were the ones who were oppressing Christians and blaspheming the name of Christ!

James must have found it to be ironic beyond measure that his readers were inclined to practise favouritism. It was because of favouritism that they were suffering persecution. The persecution had come about because the elite of society had decided that Christians were not as good as other people!

Can there be any doubt that James's letter has a lot to say to us? Ours is also a day in which Christians are increasingly being oppressed because of their faith. Why is this oppression happening? Why is it unacceptable to belittle any group in society, but Bible-believing Christians are fair game? How is it possible for a city official in a major city in the United States to declare that Christians don't belong in his city and should get out? How is it that people can speak against Christians and not be guilty of hate, but Christians cannot faithfully declare the Word of God without being charged with hate?

It is all because of this ugly thing of favouritism. Powerful segments of many societies have decided that certain minorities should be protected, and Christians are not on the list! Therefore, when we practise favouritism in the church, we are cuddling up with the very thing that is causing us so much trouble!

As is the case in every area, the Lord Jesus himself is our model. He came to this earth in our humanity to provide salvation for sinners. But he did not come only for rich, educated, powerful sinners. He came for all sinners. He came for those who are down and out as well as for those who are up and out.

And when he finally gathers his people home, there will be people of all types around the throne of God, singing, 'Worthy is the Lamb!' (Rev. 5:8–12).

Our great calling in this life is to live for the glory of the Lord Jesus, who has loved us and saved us. We do not glorify him if we are not gripped with the same spirit that brought him on his saving mission. And that was not the spirit of favouritism!

The ground is level at the foot of the cross!

FOR FURTHER STUDY

1. Read Luke 4:16–21 and 14:12–14. What do these Scriptures teach about Jesus's attitude towards the poor?

2. Read 1 Corinthians 1:26–31. What does Paul teach in this passage?

TO THINK ABOUT AND DISCUSS

1. Grade your church on the matter of treating all people equally. How can it improve in this area? What steps will you take to help your church improve?

2. Why are poor Christians rich in faith? How can you become richer in faith?

10 The folly of favouritism

(2:8–13)

James has been calling his readers, who were facing severe persecution, to live out the Word of God. Persecution has a way of making God's people see nothing but itself. In other words, persecution can cause us to be obsessed with persecution and to forget our other responsibilities. Christians are still called to live out the Word of God even when they are in the midst of difficulties. We must function as Christians in every circumstance of life.

Some of James's readers were failing in this respect. They were failing in the area of Christian love by treating others in an uneven way. Rich visitors were being warmly greeted in their church, while poor visitors were regarded as something of an inconvenience.

The whole situation was dripping with irony. James's readers were suffering persecution because the movers and shakers of their society were playing favourites, and now they themselves were doing the very same thing when they came together for worship.

In the verses of our text, James continues to deal with this business of favouritism. He does so by calling the attention of his readers to three things.

Favouritism violates God's law (vv. 8–11)

James reminds his readers of God's command: 'You shall love your neighbor as yourself' (v. 8). This command was given by God to Israel at the beginning of her existence as a nation (Lev. 19:18).

It is interesting that James refers to this as 'the royal law'. Some think that it is the royal law because it is supreme among all the other laws—the king of all God's laws. We know that love is the perfect summation of God's laws. Jesus himself taught that all the commandments of God can be summarized in terms of loving God and our fellow-man (Matt. 22:37–40). We are, therefore, on solid ground when we call God's command to love 'the king of laws'.

Others think that James had something else in mind when he used the phrase 'the royal law', namely, the nature of the one who gave this law. God is the sovereign ruler of this universe—the king of all. His laws, therefore, are to be taken seriously and obeyed.

Both interpretations are possible and in keeping with Scripture, and, in the last analysis, it doesn't matter which we embrace. James's readers knew full well what he was talking about, and they would have heartily agreed. The law of love is the royal law!

The point at issue was whether they were keeping it.

They obviously thought they were. James's charge that they were playing favourites caught them off guard. They would have responded that it was concern for the law of love that caused them to minister to the rich! And the fact that they were failing to minister to the poor was not due to lack of love. It was rather that they were so busy practising love towards the rich that they did not have any time left for anyone else. The poor man was, in the words of Gordon Keddie, 'just an unfortunate omission due to lack of time or real opportunity'.[1]

This is the reason why James uses the word 'really'. He essentially says, 'If you really fulfil the royal law, you must show love to the poor.' The law demanded no less!

James was warning his readers about the danger of selective obedience. This was the great failing of the Pharisees. They would be very scrupulous and meticulous about certain laws while ignoring all the rest.

Selective obedience fails to see the fundamental unity of the law. If we refrain from committing adultery but commit murder, we are guilty of breaking the law! Curtis Vaughan puts it like this: 'To break one link in a chain is to break the chain.'[2]

By the way, James is showing us here why we are sinners. The law of God is a code of conduct. It tells us what God wants us to do and not to do. Any failure is sin, and any sin makes us transgressors and disqualifies us from standing acceptably in God's presence.

God did not give us his laws so that we can be saved through keeping them. If that were the case, no one would be saved! God gave his laws to show us how very far short we fall of his requirements and, therefore, how desperately we need the Lord Jesus as our Saviour. The purpose of God's law is to convict us 'as transgressors' (v. 9) so we will flee to Christ.

That brings us to James's second emphasis.

Favouritism will be judged by God (v. 12)

Wherever we turn in the Bible, we find that Judgement Day is coming. The authors of the Bible lived with constant and keen awareness of the reality of that day, and, to live well, we must do the same.

James calls on his readers to live with that same awareness. He tells them to speak and act with judgement in mind. Kent Hughes writes, '"Speak" and "act" are present active imperatives: keep on speaking and keep on acting in the reality of the coming judgement.'[3]

The people to whom James wrote were guilty of favouritism because they were passing judgement on others. The cure for passing judgement on others is to remember that we must all face judgement ourselves.

> The cure for passing judgement on others is to remember that we must all face judgement ourselves.

On that great day of judgement, we will all fully realize our sins. But we will also fully realize that God's law is that which James calls it, namely, 'the law of liberty' (v. 12).

Satan has been lying about the law of God from the very beginning of human history. He has been saying all along that God's laws are designed to take the pleasure out of life, that they come from one who wants to deprive us of joy and make us miserable. It has been a very productive lie! And Satan never abandons the productive.

But on that day, his lie will be seen for what it is—a lie! And that which the Bible has been telling us all along will be abundantly and transparently clear. The laws of God were not given to bring us into a miserable bondage, but rather to bring us into glorious liberty.

If we would stop and reflect for a moment, we would see that the life of sin is that which is enslaving. The evidence is all around us.

James has one more thing to bring before his readers.

Favouritism indicates an unmerciful spirit (v. 13)

No, James was not suggesting for a single minute that we can secure salvation for ourselves by showing mercy to the poor and needy. He was much too good a theologian for that!

We are saved only by the grace of God through faith in Jesus Christ. But those who are truly saved cannot live as if they have never been touched by the mercy and grace of God. Those who know mercy cannot withhold it from others.

Curtis Vaughan offers this good summary of James's teaching:

James surely does not mean that by showing mercy to man we procure mercy from God. That would make salvation a matter of human merit and would contradict the whole tenor of Scripture.

What James means is that by failing to show compassion on our fellow men we prove ourselves to be utterly devoid of Christian character. Christian people are the children of God. They bear His image; they copy His example. It is therefore impossible for them to fail to share in His compassion, to fail to reflect His spirit of mercy.[4]

Those who have truly been saved will give evidence of the merciful character of the God who saved them. As they give that evidence, they will assure themselves that they truly have been saved and, therefore, have nothing to fear on the Day of Judgement. 'Mercy triumphs over judgment' (v. 13).

For further study ▶

FOR FURTHER STUDY

1. Read Matthew 23:23. What example did Jesus give of the Pharisees' selective obedience?

2. Read Romans 14:12 and Hebrews 9:27–28. What do these verses teach us about God's judgement?

TO THINK ABOUT AND DISCUSS

1. What examples of selective obedience can you see in today's evangelical church?

2. What can you do to develop a more merciful spirit?

11 The danger of dead faith

(2:14–19)

James is elaborating on the three marks of true religion. He is dealing with caring for the needy. He has said that we cannot do this if we are guilty of the revolting sin of favouritism.

Now he is saying that we cannot dodge this caring ministry if we have true faith. True faith will not allow us to walk through life without caring and ministering. And if we think otherwise, we do not have true faith!

We can divide James's teaching on this matter into five sections.

Two arresting questions (v. 14)

There is not much point in saying something if no one is listening. James wants to make sure his readers are listening! So he does not begin by saying that he has done considerable research on a matter and is now ready to present his findings. No, not at all! He rather begins by asking a couple of questions, the second of which is: 'Can faith save him?'

Now there are certain statements that are so universally held among Christians that to deny them is to brand oneself as a non-Christian. 'Jesus is Lord' is one such statement. 'Salvation is by grace through faith' is another. And now James, the half-brother of Jesus himself, has the audacity to question whether faith saves! James has their attention!

Having secured it, he presses on to ...

A hypothetical situation (vv. 15–16)

James calls his readers to imagine themselves being confronted by a brother or sister in Christ who is 'naked and destitute of daily food' (v. 15).

Such a situation demands a response, and someone has a response. While the church is gazing upon the scene of urgent and crying need, one person pipes up, 'Depart in peace, be warmed and filled' (v. 16).

The individual has expressed the commendable desire to see the needs of this brother or sister met. But have any needs been met? Has anything changed? No, the brother or sister is still naked and hungry! All that has taken place is that some words have been spoken.

Mere words are worthless if they do not lead to action, and, therefore, faith is useless if it is nothing more than a matter of words!

That brings us to the next section.

A conclusion (v. 17)

Having read James's words about the needy brother or sister, the people to whom James wrote waited for the other foot to fall. And fall it did! James writes, 'Thus also faith by itself, if it does not have works, is dead' (v. 17).

James's words have sparked a tremendous debate. Is James really denying salvation by faith? Is he really suggesting that salvation can be secured only by producing good works? Is James out of step with the great apostle Paul, who so loudly trumpeted and heroically championed the doctrine of salvation by faith?

The answer to each of these questions is a resounding 'No!' James was not denying salvation by faith. He was not advocating salvation by works. He was not disagreeing with the apostle Paul.

James believed firmly in salvation by faith, but he believed just as firmly that saving faith inevitably shows up in good works. Kent Hughes helpfully explains, 'Paul's teaching about faith and works focuses on the time *before* conversion, and James's focus is *after* conversion' (italics are his).[1]

We do not have a works faith, but we believe that faith works. We might say that good works cannot produce salvation, but salvation most certainly produces good works. John Calvin says, 'It is faith alone that justifies, but faith that justifies can never be alone.'[2]

> Good works cannot produce salvation, but salvation most certainly produces good works.

James is really dealing here, then, with a very common problem, namely, thinking we have true faith without really having it. He is dealing with the matter of being deceived about salvation. Notice again his questions in verse 14:

'What does it profit, my brethren, if someone says he has faith but does not have works? Can faith save him?'

The emphasis is on a person saying that he or she has faith. But the absence of works from that person's life proves that this faith is a matter of words only.

James is making the same point that the apostle John made: 'My little children, let us not love in word or in tongue, but in deed and in truth' (1 John 3:18). He would also have us remember the words of the Lord Jesus: 'Let your light so shine before men, that they may see your good works and glorify your Father in heaven' (Matt. 5:16).

Having drawn his conclusion, James proceeds to handle ...

An objection (v. 18)

James was a splendid reader of people. He knew that some would respond to his teaching by suggesting that it was just a matter of emphasis. A Christian over here specializes in faith, and one over there specializes in works. But both are true Christians!

James will have none of it! He maintains that it is impossible to show faith without works, but it is possible to show faith through works. Kent Hughes observes, 'Faith and works are like the wings of a bird. There can be no real life, no flight, with a single wing, whether works or faith. But when the two are pumping together in concert, their owner soars through the heavens.'[3]

James wraps up this section by making ...

A searching comparison (v. 19)

We are saved only by faith in the redeeming work of the Lord

Jesus. Let us never be mistaken about that! But there is such a thing as true faith, and there is such a thing as false faith. One of the marks of false faith is that it contents itself with mere belief in the existence of God.

James's readers were Jews who had been converted to Christianity. Their Jewish background meant that they were very familiar with the 'Shema', the Jewish confession of faith: 'Hear, O Israel: The Lord our God, the Lord is one!'

Is it good to believe that there is one God? Absolutely! James says that those who believe this truth 'do well'. But is belief in the existence of God sufficient for the saving of the soul? James answers by pointing to the demons of hell. They also believe in God! They know the truth about God, and the truth they know makes them 'tremble', or 'shudder'. It makes them 'bristle up' like a frightened cat![4]

But is their belief saving belief? Of course not! And neither is our belief in God, if it consists of nothing more than nodding in agreement with various propositions and statements about God.

Gordon Keddie writes of the demons,

They actually have a more informed 'faith' than human hypocrites! Men and women can make their easy professions of faith and live their worldly lives as if there were not God at all. Their casual blasphemies about 'the man upstairs' can roll off their tongues with never the slightest tremble at the consequences of offending a sovereign and holy God! Why is it that demons tremble, while sinners sail on in blissful unconcern? The answer is that the demons are not so blind as people. They know their latter end … They really fear the wrath to come. But careless sinners say they believe in God positively, go on in daily life to live as if he did not exist and yet can dream that they are safe in the everlasting arms![5]

Posing arresting questions, creating a hypothetical situation, stating a firm conclusion, handling an objection and drawing a startling comparison—James has put his readers through their paces and us through ours.

Have we heard the man? Have we allowed him to convince us? Faith must show up in our lives. If it doesn't, it is because it is not there!

FOR FURTHER STUDY

1. Read Ephesians 2:8–10. What does Paul say about faith and works?
2. Read John 14:21–24. What does Jesus identify as the mark of those who truly love him?

TO THINK ABOUT AND DISCUSS

1. What evidence can you see in your life that you have true faith in the Lord?
2. What do you regard as signs of a mere intellectual belief as opposed to true belief in the Lord?

12 Proving faith by works

(2:20–26)

In these verses James continues to warn his readers about the danger of a dead faith, that is, one which claims to believe in the Lord Jesus but gives no evidence of it.

How very much we need this warning! I do not hesitate to say that this is the major problem in churches today. Multitudes have walked an aisle, stood before a congregation and professed to believe in the Lord Jesus. They have been baptized and placed on the membership roll. All would seem to be well—but it is not! These same people do not attend the services of the church, do not give anything to support its ministry and do not take up any of its responsibilities. They show no interest in ministering to the needy. On the other hand, they are very much like unbelievers, holding the same values, going to the same places and speaking in the same way.

What are we to say about such people? Many would say that the problem is that the church in which these people made their profession and were baptized made no attempt to 'follow up' or to disciple them. The people themselves are truly Christians, but they give no sign of it because of the church's failure.

Others attempt to explain the problem through what is known as 'the carnal Christian' teaching. This teaching maintains that these people are truly saved because they have accepted Jesus as Saviour. But they are not living as they should because they have not yet accepted Jesus as their Lord. He is in their lives, but he is not yet on the throne of their hearts! These people have the best of both worlds. They are saved and, therefore, get to go to heaven when they die, but they live as if they were lost.

To all of this James gives a very plain and resounding answer—faith without works is dead! The problem with those who give no evidence of faith, James says, is nothing less than this: they do not possess true faith.

Having stated this teaching, James turns in these verses to give two examples of it. These examples come from the Old Testament. The first concerns the patriarch Abraham. The second concerns the prostitute Rahab.

The patriarch Abraham (vv. 21–24)

Every Bible student knows that sinners are justified (declared guiltless before God) by faith in the redeeming work of the Lord Jesus. And the Bible tells us that Abraham was justified by faith (Gen. 15:6; Rom. 4:20–22). But here James says Abraham was justified by works (v. 21)!

To prove his point, James refers to the time when God commanded Abraham to sacrifice his son Isaac (Gen.

22:1–14). We know the story well. God had promised to make Abraham the father of a great nation, but for years he had no son. Finally, God gave Isaac to Abraham and Sarah, and Isaac was designated as the one from whom that nation would come (Gen. 21:12).

But then, suddenly and inexplicably, Abraham was told to sacrifice Isaac! It was a test of Abraham's faith, and Abraham passed the test. He was given two seemingly contradictory words. One word was that Isaac had to live in order for the promise of a nation to be fulfilled. The other was that Isaac had to die. Instead of believing one word and rejecting the other, Abraham believed both! He believed the promise that Isaac would be the one through whom the nation would come, and yet obeyed the command to sacrifice Isaac, believing as he did that, if necessary, God would raise Isaac from the dead (Heb. 11:17–19).

Why did James cite this particular episode? Did James actually believe that Abraham himself was saved from his sins because he was willing to sacrifice Isaac? Is that the reason why he says Abraham was justified by works?

James believed no such thing! He had read his Old Testament well and knew that Abraham was actually declared righteous ('justified') by God long before he was called to sacrifice Isaac (Gen. 15:6).

His willingness to sacrifice Isaac was, therefore, not the means by which he secured salvation. He already possessed that! It was rather Abraham showing by his obedience that he truly had faith.

James's point is plain. Just as Abraham showed that he

had faith by his works, so his readers were to do the same. And we are to be doing the same as well.

That brings us to James's second illustration.

The prostitute Rahab (v. 25)

For his second example, James cites the story of Rahab, who was a prostitute in the city of Jericho.

Are you wondering how James got from Abraham to Rahab? From the patriarch to the prostitute? James did so because he was anticipating an objection. He knew that some of his readers would respond to the illustration of Abraham along these lines: 'James, you're telling us to show our faith by our works. And you're citing Abraham! That isn't fair! Everyone knows that Abraham was a special man. Surely you do not expect us to be like him?'

James reaches, as it were, to the opposite end of the spectrum, and he does so to make the very same point: true faith evidences itself in good works.

We remember this story. Joshua and the people of Israel were about to begin their conquest of the land of Canaan. The city of Jericho was the first and most intimidating target. Joshua, shrewd military man that he was, sent spies into the city (Josh. 2:1). They went to the house of Rahab because they thought that it would not arouse suspicion for strangers to go to the house of a prostitute.

But they were mistaken. The king of Jericho got word that spies had come to the city and were at the house of Rahab (Josh. 2:2). The king immediately sent men to search for the spies, but Rahab hid them (Josh. 2:3–7) and enabled them to escape (Josh. 2:15–16).

We must ask the same question we posed when we were considering what James had to say about Abraham: Is James saying that Rahab secured salvation for herself by doing the good work of helping Israel's spies?

And we must arrive at the same answer we got when we were considering Abraham. No! Abraham had been saved by faith long before he was called to offer Isaac. The offering of Isaac was not, therefore, the means by which he secured faith. It was rather the means by which he expressed or manifested his faith.

It is exactly the same with Rahab. She already possessed faith before the spies ever came to her. Here is part of what she said to the spies when they arrived: '… the LORD your God, He is God in heaven above and on earth beneath' (Josh. 2:11). Word about Israel and her God had come to Rahab and the other inhabitants of Jericho before the spies ever came. And Rahab had believed that word (Josh. 2:9–14). What she did with the spies was, then, a result of the faith that already existed in her heart.

But the point is that both Abraham and Rahab *did* something! They did not just claim to have faith in God and sit idly. Their faith led them to action. And true faith has not changed in all the centuries that have come and gone since Abraham and Rahab. It still leads to action.

Faith which does not produce works is not really faith at all! Curtis Vaughan rightly says, 'Faith

> Curtis Vaughan rightly says, 'Faith which does not produce works is therefore comparable to a corpse.'

which does not produce works is therefore comparable to a corpse.'[1] Martin Luther says of faith, 'Oh, it is a living, busy, active, mighty thing, this faith; and so it is impossible for it not to do good works incessantly. It does not ask whether there are good works to do, but before the question rises; it has already done them, and is always at the doing of them. He who does not these works is a faithless man.'[2]

For further study ▶

FOR FURTHER STUDY

1. Read Hebrews 11:7. What work did Noah do because of his faith?
2. Read Hebrews 11:23–27. What did Moses do because of his faith?

TO THINK ABOUT AND DISCUSS

1. How does your church typically explain the lack of interest in spiritual things among church members?
2. What is the proper response for a person who belongs to a church that does not have a biblical understanding of the above question?

13 Three notes

(3:1–2)

Those to whom James wrote his epistle were very concerned about the persecution that was coming their way because of their faith in Christ. James was concerned about their suffering as well, but he was more concerned about the genuineness of their faith. It was as if he was saying to his readers: it is far more important that you have real faith than that you are suffering.

But how could his readers tell if they had real faith? James gave them three marks: controlling the tongue, caring for the needy and avoiding worldliness (1:26–27).

In the verses of our text, James begins to elaborate and expand on this matter of controlling the tongue. These two verses are preliminary or introductory in nature. As we examine them, we can identify three notes.

A note of caution (v. 1)

This note may well come as a shock to most of us. There are so many things that James could have cautioned his readers about, and the thing he chooses is teaching!

He writes, 'My brethren, let not many of you become teachers …' (v. 1). We have a hard time believing that James would say such a thing because we know how very difficult it is for most churches to find enough teachers. This is a verse that many pastors and leaders would prefer to keep hidden. But it is here, and we must not ignore it.

Why did James think it necessary to include this? We can safely say that he had no desire to make it harder for churches to find teachers. Rather he was warning his readers about the terrible possibility of taking up the task of teaching with the wrong motive.

In those times, much dignity and acclaim came to those who were teachers. The people in those days were taught to regard teachers with utmost respect.

Citing William Barclay, Kent Hughes offers this explanation: 'The title rabbi meant "My great one", and those holding that office were accorded the greatest respect. One's duty to help a rabbi exceeded even the duty to help one's parents. In fact, should a rabbi and one's father and mother be captured by an enemy, duty demanded that the rabbi be ransomed first!'[1]

Such respect for teachers created a temptation for many to take up the task so that they might receive the fawning of an adoring public.

Our appeal, then, to all who are interested in teaching is

simply this: by all means, take up the work, but make sure you are doing it for the right reason. We are not to teach to satisfy our own ego needs, but to bring glory to God and to deliver his Word accurately to the eternal benefit of those who hear us.

> We are not to teach to satisfy our own ego needs, but to bring glory to God and to deliver his Word accurately to the eternal benefit of those who hear us.

We cannot leave this point without noting the reason James attached to this note of caution, namely, stricter judgement (v. 1). It is an awesome thing to stand before eternity-bound people to unfold and explain the Word of God! I sometimes find myself shuddering as I think of the magnitude and seriousness of the task. And I shudder as I observe so many who go about the task with flippancy and lightness, conducting themselves as mere entertainers who are out to get a laugh.

I also shudder when I hear about teachers who have such little regard for their task that they do not adequately prepare, or they use the time set apart for the teaching of the Word of God to discuss mere trivialities.

I shudder when I hear teachers and preachers joke about things that are sacred. And I shudder when I hear a person set aside the clear teaching of the Bible so that he or she can be in line with current thinking.

There are many, many ways in which we can misuse our tongues—blasphemy, lying, gossiping, profanity—but none could possibly be more serious than using them to misrepresent and distort the Word of God!

We had better know this very well: God takes the teaching of his Word seriously, and so should we! If we doubt that God takes the matter seriously, we need only read Paul's words in 1 Corinthians 3:10–15. He tells us that teachers can build with gold, silver and precious stones or with wood, hay and stubble. The coming day of judgement will reveal the kind of work that we have done, and those who have built with the wood, hay and stubble will see their work utterly consumed and will realize that they have accomplished absolutely nothing!

We cannot leave this point without paying tribute to those teachers who have served so faithfully and diligently. Poor teachers do much harm, but who can calculate the good achieved by conscientious teachers? Eternity itself will finally reveal the value of such teachers.

A note of realism (v. 2)

Having offered the note of caution about rushing heedlessly into the teaching of God's Word, James proceeds to observe that 'we all stumble in many things'.

James doesn't want us to misconstrue his words about teaching. Yes, it is a serious business, but we must not allow ourselves to go to the extreme to which some have gone, excusing ourselves from the work of the Lord because we are imperfect.

In all of human history, there has only been one person who did the work of God perfectly, and that was the Lord Jesus Christ. Our plea is not for perfect people to go about the work of teaching, it is rather for imperfect people to go about the work in a serious and diligent way, praying, as they do so, that the Lord will be pleased to use them in their weakness. We plead for people to join the apostle Paul in his understanding that we are mere earthen vessels (2 Cor. 4:7) and to say with him, 'Not that we are sufficient of ourselves to think of anything as being from ourselves, but our sufficiency is from God' (2 Cor. 3:5).

A note of hope (v. 2)

James is about to go into some detail about the importance of controlling the tongue. We will find what he has to say to be very challenging and distressing. But before he goes further, he holds out some hope for us: 'If anyone does not stumble in word, he is a perfect man, able also to bridle the whole body' (v. 2).

The word 'perfect' refers to maturity. James was saying that those who control their speech are well on the way to spiritual maturity.

Every Christian is interested in spiritual maturity. No one can be a Christian and not be interested in growing in the things of the Lord.

James gives us some valuable guidance. He essentially says, 'Do you want to achieve spiritual maturity? Concentrate on your talking! If you can get this under control, the rest will be relatively easy for you.' He does not say that spiritual maturity is impossible. Nor does he say it is easy. Here is the note of hope—it is possible! And the way to begin achieving it is by giving special attention to our speech.

For further study ▶

FOR FURTHER STUDY

1. Read Matthew 23:6–12. What does Jesus say about the teaching of the Pharisees?
2. Read 2 Timothy 2:1–7, 14–16 and 4:1–5. What does Paul teach about teaching?

TO THINK ABOUT AND DISCUSS

1. What can you do to encourage faithful teachers in their work?
2. How can you tell if the teaching you are receiving is good and sound?

14 The trouble with the tongue

(3:3–12)

In these verses, James continues to deal with the issue of controlling the tongue. Have you ever wondered why James saw fit to include this section? We know that he wrote his letter to encourage and instruct Christians who were facing persecution. And here we have him sounding a warning about the use of the tongue.

We can safely assume that James wrote along these lines because his readers had been speaking irresponsibly. Perhaps they had been complaining about their circumstances. Or maybe they had been complaining about each other and criticizing each other. The fact that a Christian is undergoing persecution does not mean that he or she is perfect. It doesn't mean that there is no struggle with the same things with which non-persecuted Christians struggle.

The truth is that our difficulties can make us less careful

about sin. The fact that we are going through hardships can make us think that we 'deserve a break' and that we are entitled to take a few liberties.

James wanted his readers to know that the persecution they were enduring did not give them the right to throw off all restraint. It did not give them the right to talk as if they were not Christians. The persecution gave them the opportunity to show the difference that their Christianity had made in their lives, but they could not do this if they were talking irresponsibly.

But James was also aware of the enormous difficulty of controlling the tongue, and that is what he emphasizes in these verses.

The power of the tongue (vv. 3–8)

He first points out that the tongue, although it is very small, is extremely powerful. He drives this point home by calling attention to three large things that are affected or controlled by very small things.

- The horse is a very large and powerful animal, but it is easily controlled by a very small thing—the bit in its mouth (v. 3).
- A ship is also a very large and powerful thing, but it is easily controlled by something that is quite small—the rudder (v. 4).
- A forest can be a very large thing, sprawling over thousands of acres, but the whole thing can be destroyed by an untended campfire (v. 5).

James's point is not hard to see. The bit, the rudder and the campfire all have power that is out of proportion to their size. And the power that James has in mind is the power to destroy! The mention of the little fire that leads to the forest being destroyed leads James to say, 'And the tongue is a fire' (v. 6).

We know it is true. The tongue, a mere two ounces of membrane, can bring incalculable ruin and wreckage. We easily call to mind Adolf Hitler, who used his tongue to whip a whole nation into an emotional frenzy that led to millions of deaths in World War II.

But we must not be content to apply James's words only to mad political leaders. Everybody who has a tongue has the power to create destruction and havoc.

How many churches have been ruined by gossip and slander! How many individuals have had their reputations ruined because of such talk! People who would never think about setting fire to their neighbour's house can and do commit spiritual arson!

Where does the tongue get its fire? Where does it get its power to destroy and burn? James leaves no doubt at all about this. He says the tongue is 'set on fire by hell' (v. 6). Kent Hughes says, 'The uncontrolled tongue has a direct pipeline to Hell!'[1] He also suggests that the flow in that pipeline goes both ways. Irresponsible talk comes from hell, and it helps fill hell! How many are in hell today because they heard hellacious talk from professing Christians?

And what is hellacious talk? We must most certainly include that which I have already mentioned—gossip and slander. But we must also include blasphemy, profanity, complaining, criticizing and innuendo.

Having emphasized the destructive power of the

little tongue, James proceeds to assert that it is virtually untameable (vv. 7–8). He finds himself thinking of man's success in taming the various animals. Elephants, crocodiles, sea creatures, birds—all can be tamed or controlled with comparative ease. A man can stand in front of the massive lion, crack a whip, bark a command, and the lion obeys! But that same man can stand in front of a mirror, stick out his tongue, crack his whip, and the tongue goes right on talking and destroying!

James says the tongue is 'an unruly evil, full of deadly poison' (v. 8). According to him, there is such a thing as 'verbal cyanide', which does its killing work before its presence can even be detected.[2]

And James is not yet done. He also wants his readers to see ...

The remarkably inconsistent nature of the tongue (vv. 9–12)

The tongue is the little hypocrite in our mouths that can make big hypocrites out of us.

> The tongue is the little hypocrite in our mouths that can make big hypocrites out of us.

Here is the hypocrisy of the tongue: one minute it is blessing God, and the very next minute it is cursing men who have been made in the image of God (v. 9).

James considered this to be quite remarkable. A spring of water cannot produce both fresh and bitter water (v. 11). And a fig tree cannot produce both figs and olives. A grapevine cannot produce both grapes and figs (v. 12). But the tongue can produce both blessing and cursing!

And, faced with this grand inconsistency, James can only say, 'My brethren, these things ought not to be so' (v. 10).

And we know James is right! We know that our irresponsible and inconsistent talking is not right. And yet we go on and on and on because of the unruly, untameable nature of the tongue.

Left to ourselves, we cannot tame the tongue, but, thank God, we who know the Lord are not left to ourselves. The Lord has given us his Word to guide us and his Spirit to indwell us. And what do the guiding Word and indwelling Spirit tell us to do about our tongues?

Repent

First, they tell us to repent of all our wrong talking. We all have much of which to repent, for, as James says, 'we all stumble in many things' (v. 2).

But let us know that, while sinful talking is serious, repentance brings God's forgiveness and removes our sins as far from us as the east is from the west.

Count the cost

We must also make it our daily business to think long and hard on the terrible cost attached to sinful talking and determine that we shall set a seal on our lips (Ps. 39:1) so that nothing that is unwholesome will pass through. And we must ask the Lord to help us keep that resolve, knowing that we will certainly never be able to keep it apart from him.

Speak good

We must also make it our business to fill our mouths with

good things. The more our mouths are filled with praise to God and good, kind and encouraging words regarding others, the less space there will be for fiery, poisonous talk.

Look to the Lord

Finally, we must continually look to the Lord Jesus Christ, who is our example in all things. We know how very hard it is to control our tongues. What a marvel it is that the Lord Jesus perfectly controlled his, never speaking a wrong word! Because of his perfect obedience to the Lord God, we who have no righteousness of our own can be clothed in his. How very thankful we should be for this!

> May the mind of Christ my Saviour
> Live in me from day to day,
> By His love and pow'r controlling
> All I do and say.
>
> (Kate B. Wilkinson)

FOR FURTHER STUDY

1. Read Proverbs 21:23. What does this verse teach about controlling the tongue?
2. Read Proverbs 15:1–4. What do these verses teach about the tongue?

TO THINK ABOUT AND DISCUSS

1. Do a tongue inventory. How frequently do you complain, criticize, gossip, lie, etc.?
2. What steps can you take to improve your speaking?

15 Who is driving your car?

(3:13–18)

I don't want to insult you, but I do wonder if you have ever thought of yourself as a car and your life as a road? You are aware, are you not, that you are moving along? You are not stationary. You are not the same age today as you were yesterday! You surely must be aware that you are moving towards a destination. The journey you are on will eventually end!

A nd you must also realize that, just like your car, you sometimes break down! You sometimes need to be adjusted, and you sometimes need repair. And how about this—you sometimes run into other cars!

There are other parallels as well. We sometimes move along at a pretty good clip, and at other times we barely creep along. We sometimes hit bumps, and we sometimes hit the ditch!

If you are willing to admit that you are like a car, I have

a question for you: Who is driving you? You might think your spouse, your kids or your boss is doing the driving. But the Bible tells us that there are only two possible drivers for our cars. James identifies them in the verses of our text. One driver is false wisdom, and the other is true wisdom.

False wisdom (vv. 13–16)

James did not know anything about cars, but he did know about his readers. He could see that they were in danger of being driven by the wrong kind of wisdom.

Some of them were taking up the teaching role in the church (v. 1), and were doing so for all the wrong reasons. Charles Erdman calls them 'self-appointed teachers who were proud of boasted knowledge, who were fond of dispute, who were bitter in their discussions, who were more eager to defeat their opponents than to establish the truth'.[1]

Some were using their tongues in a very hurtful and harmful way, without regard to the damage that they were doing. Furthermore, as James looked at them, he could see 'bitter envy' and a 'self-seeking' boastfulness (v. 14).

Imagine it! Taking up the teaching role because they were envious of others and because they wanted to advance themselves! Cutting others down for the same reasons!

Teachers of the Bible are to be advancing the truth. That should be their motive. But because they were fuelled by envy and self-centredness, these people were 'lying against the truth' (v. 14). They were working against the very truth they were supposed to be conveying!

In the verses of our text, James traces all these tendencies back to their root. He essentially says to them, 'Do you know why you are doing these things? Do you know why you are misusing the teaching office and why you are cutting up others with your words? It is because you are being driven along by false wisdom.'

What kind of wisdom is this? James is ready with the answer. He calls it 'earthly', 'sensual' and 'demonic' (v. 15).

What does 'earthly' mean? It means that this false wisdom of which James is speaking has this world as its boundaries. It begins and ends with this world. It does not consider eternity. James's point is obvious. When they were teaching for the wrong reasons and speaking in the wrong way, they were thinking like people of earth instead of people of heaven!

The word 'sensual' refers to our fleshly appetites. Once again, James is very clear. When his readers were teaching for the wrong reasons and speaking in the wrong way, they were doing so to gratify their own desires. They were thinking of no one but themselves.

> The devil does not come to us as he is often portrayed, that is, as an ugly, ferocious creature. As James says, he comes in the garb of wisdom.

Then James adds the word 'demonic'. He has traced what his readers had been doing to false wisdom. Now he traces false wisdom to the devil.

When we allow ourselves to be driven by false wisdom, we are allowing Satan to slip into the driver's seat!

Some seem to think there is no way that the devil can drive them. If they see him coming, they will just lock the doors! But the devil does not come to us as he is often portrayed, that is, as an ugly, ferocious creature. As James says, he comes in the garb of wisdom.

James is not yet through with his devastating analysis of devilish wisdom. He wraps it up by saying that it leads to 'confusion and every evil thing' (v. 16). We have already said that cars sometimes hit the ditch. That is where this false wisdom winds up!

There is, then, a kind of wisdom that fills us with ourselves and makes us very proud of ourselves. It's obvious that a lot of people are being driven by this kind of 'wisdom'! Tragically, it is possible for Christians to let this driver slide behind the wheel!

What a terrible thing it is to be driven along by false wisdom! How very thankful we should be that there is another driver for the car of life, namely, the Lord himself. The Lord drives through ...

True wisdom (vv. 17–18)

This is the wisdom of God. It is 'the wisdom that is from above' (v. 17). It is wisdom that springs from God and pertains to God.

What is this wisdom like? James says:

- It is 'pure'. This means it is free from all the things that characterize false wisdom.
- It is also 'peaceable'. It delights in peace and promotes peace.
- It is 'gentle'. It is not combative and abrasive. It is reasonable and courteous.
- It is 'willing to yield'. It is open to reason. It doesn't insist on its rights and its own way.

- It is 'full of mercy', that is, it shows compassion to those who are in need.
- It is 'full of ... good fruits'. That means it is rich in good deeds.
- It is 'without partiality'. It does not show favouritism.
- It is 'without hypocrisy'. It is sincere and genuine. It doesn't put on a front.

This is God's wisdom, and when we allow this wisdom to drive us down the road of life—which is another way of saying we allow God to drive us—we achieve a wonderful result. That result is righteousness (v. 18). Righteousness is, of course, right conduct. It is right living, that is, living in accordance with the will of God.

There is a sequence here. Right living is the result of people of peace sowing seeds of peace. And the people of peace are those who are driven by true wisdom.

James has put quite a challenge before us. At every point of our lives, and especially in our speaking, we who know the Lord have the opportunity to demonstrate that we are functioning on the basis of wisdom from above.

As we demonstrate that wisdom, we have reason to believe that unbelievers will take note and will themselves desire to have wisdom from God. And when they express that desire, we can point them to the Lord Jesus Christ, who is himself 'wisdom from God' (1 Cor. 1:30).

Jesus is God's wise way of providing forgiveness of sins and eternal glory for all who receive him as their Lord and Saviour.

The other side of the coin is this: with every opportunity, there is a danger. The danger is that we who know the

Lord will not seize the opportunities to demonstrate divine wisdom, but will rather reflect worldly wisdom. Because that danger is always very present and real, we must each day pray, 'Lord, let me this day be driven by your wisdom.'

For further study ▶

FOR FURTHER STUDY

1. Read Psalm 1:1–3. How do these verses depict the person who is driven by the wisdom of God?

2. Read Psalm 1:4–6. How do these verses depict the person who is driven by false wisdom?

TO THINK ABOUT AND DISCUSS

1. What indications do you see that many churches are being driven by false wisdom?

2. What can you do to help children distinguish between false wisdom and true wisdom and to be driven by the latter?

16 The 'ness' mess

(4:1–6)

Christians are supposed to be singing from the same hymn sheet. We are supposed to believe that we came into this world with a sinful nature, and that that sinful nature made us unworthy to enter God's presence and deserving of God's wrath.

We are supposed to believe that we are absolutely incapable of doing anything to help ourselves, and that we are saved because God had mercy on us and sent his Son to die in our stead and his Holy Spirit to regenerate our dead hearts.

We are supposed to love the persons of the triune God above everything else. We are supposed to have a passion for the worship of God and the service of God.

We are supposed to believe that we are to do all we can to advance the cause of God. We are supposed to believe that we are to do all we can to influence our children to love and

> The sad fact is that many church members appear to be working against the very things they are supposed to value and prize.

serve God. We are supposed to believe that we are to do all we can to influence our friends and neighbours for Christ.

But as we survey modern-day Christianity, we are compelled to admit that many of those who profess to be believers do not appear to be in agreement. We are supposed to believe these things, but many do not give any evidence of doing so. The sad fact is that many church members appear to be working against the very things they are supposed to value and prize.

Why is this the case? I suggest that much of the reason lies in 'the "ness" mess'.

We can find this phenomenon in the verses of our text. As James looked at his readers, he could see three things that were holding them back. We see the same things in our churches.

Quarrelsomeness (vv. 1–2a)

James's look at the church caused him to see a very shocking and disturbing thing—a divided church!

Is there anything sadder than such a church? The church is to be united in love for God and love for one another. The church is to be united around the truth of God. The church is to be united in worship and service.

But here was a divided church! James could see 'wars' and 'fights' among them. The former suggests ongoing hostility; the latter suggests brief outbursts of antagonism.

Ongoing hostility! Bursts of antagonism! In the church? Say it isn't so! But it was so in that church, and it is so in many churches today.

What was feeding this quarrelsomeness that James saw? It was another member of the 'ness' family—selfishness! The people were going to church for the wrong reason—not to help the church and advance it, but to advance themselves. Each wanted to be known as somebody. Each was seeking his or her own good instead of the good of brothers and sisters in Christ. Each was named 'Diotrephes' in that each one sought the pre-eminence.

This lust for prominence led them to 'murder' one another. No, things had not deteriorated to the point that they were actually drawing their swords in worship and hacking one another to death! But that lust had led them to hate one another, and hatred is inward murder.

How can such a church advance the cause of Christ? It can't. A church filled with anger and strife refutes its own message. It says to unbelievers, 'Come to Christ, and he will change your life.' And the unbelievers all around laugh and say, 'Why is it that he has not changed you?'

> A church filled with anger and strife refutes its own message.

On the night before he was crucified, the Lord Jesus spoke these words to his disciples: 'A new commandment I give to you, that you love one another; as I have loved you, that you also love one another. By this all will know that you are My disciples, if you have love for one another' (John 13:34–35). But what if the world does not see that love? There is only one conclusion left for the world to draw: these people are not disciples of Christ!

How very easy it is for us to fail here! How very easy it is to come to church to promote ourselves instead of Christ! How very difficult it is for us to see ourselves as we are!

To the evil of quarrelsomeness, James now adds ...

Prayerlessness (vv. 2b–3)

James's people needed their 'wants' fixed. They were wanting the wrong things as they came to church. They were wanting their own desires gratified.

There is nothing wrong with wanting things if the things we want are good and right. And if they are good and right, there is a way for us to get what we want—through prayer!

If we come to the church wanting prestige, we will pound on one another. If we come to the church wanting the Lord to be glorified and our fellow-Christians edified, we will pray for one another.

Because these people wanted the wrong things, they could not ask God for the right things. And because they were not asking God for the right things, they were not receiving anything from God; '... you do not have because you do not ask,' James says.

This was not only a terrible indictment of them, it is also a terrible indictment of us. We do not have because we do not ask!

One of the questions that I have frequently been asked over the years concerns unanswered prayer. Why does God not answer our prayers? I tell you that there is a far greater problem in our churches. It is the problem of unasked prayer!

Once again, we are supposed to be in agreement! We are supposed to believe that nothing is more important for the kingdom of God than prayer, but how many of us are truly giving it priority?

James could not let his readers get away from the matter of prayer without also linking it to that nasty member of the 'ness' family he introduced earlier. Selfishness is here also! It shows up in the prayer closet! We come to God ostensibly to seek his glory, and we end up seeking our own, offering as our petitions those things that will make life more comfortable and convenient for us (v. 3). How many of us have ever prayed for God to put us through the wringer if, in so doing, he can gain greater glory for himself?

It would be OK with me if James had not gone any further. He has given me quite enough to ponder and absorb. But the man will not let up! He introduces yet another member of the 'ness' clan …

Worldliness (vv. 4–6)

Pastors today are terrified at the thought of offending their people. James didn't concern himself with that. He calls them 'adulterers and adulteresses'!

He affirms that they were giving to someone else the love and devotion that belonged to God and God alone. Who was this rival lover? It was the world. These people were more in love with their world than they were with God!

The 'world' is James's term for life that is lived as if this present world were all that there is. It is life that is lived without regard to God. It is life that is lived according to the values, desires and aspirations of this temporal realm. What is worldliness? It is thinking like the world, talking like the world, acting like the world, and dressing like the world.

This is the day of 'worldly Christians'. But the problem is that true Christians cannot be continually worldly. Yes, Christians can and do slip into worldly behaviour from time to time. But that is a far cry from habitual worldliness. If the pattern of our lives is worldliness, we have plain evidence that we are deceived about our relationship with God.

> This is the day of 'worldly Christians'. But the problem is that true Christians cannot be continually worldly.

The reason why the Christian cannot be habitually worldly is plain to see. James maintains that God has put in his people 'the Spirit' who 'yearns jealously' (v. 5). The Holy Spirit of God who earnestly desires that we give our devotion entirely to God will not let us go on in sin without running riot in our consciences!

And the same Lord who yearns for us gives us grace (v. 6). The world would prove to be too strong for us if the Lord of grace did not grant us grace for living in it. If we humbly seek his grace, he will not fail to give it. If we proudly reject it, God will set himself in battle array against us.

Many churches and individual Christians are in the clutches of these cut-throat 'nesses'—quarrelsomeness, prayerlessness and worldliness. And the nastiest 'ness' of all—selfishness—is behind them. The way to defeat these villains is to cry out to God to help us. What good could our churches do if they could get free of these enemies?

For further study ▶

FOR FURTHER STUDY

1. Read 1 John 3:10–15. What does John tell us about loving our fellow-Christians?
2. Read Psalm 66:18; Proverbs 28:9; Isaiah 59:1–3. What do these verses teach about prayer?

TO THINK ABOUT AND DISCUSS

1. Do a 'ness' inventory. Which 'ness' has the firmest grip on your life? What can you do to break that grip?
2. Take steps to get a small group of believers to pray with you for the thing that will break the 'ness' grip in our churches and individual lives: revival!

17 The cure for worldliness

(4:7–10)

All Scripture is inspired by God, and it is all profitable to us in some way or other. But there are some Scriptures that are more needed and relevant at given points in the life of the church than others.

I doubt that we can find a passage which the church needs more than the one we have before us. This passage gives us the cure for 'world-infected Christians.'[1] We desperately need this cure.

The first part of it is …

Submitting to the authority of God (vv. 7–8a)

Is there anything more vexing than a child who refuses to submit to his or her parents? When told to do something, the child obstinately refuses. When told not to do something, he or she immediately does it! We all detest rebellion in children, especially when we see it coming from children who have exceptionally good parents.

Do we detest that same rebellion in ourselves? Even the best parents are flawed in many ways, but the Lord is perfect in every way. And from the coffer of his goodness, he has poured out upon us blessing after blessing. How are we responding to these things? Are we doing what the Lord tells us to do? Are we refraining from those things he tells us not to do? Are we submitting to the Lord, or are we acting as ungrateful, rebellious children?

Rebellion against God is a serious matter. The devil is the greatest rebel of all time, and he is in the business of persuading God's people to join him in rebellion. If, then, we are rebelling against God, we are submitting to the devil.

> The devil really is something of a coward. When he sees the people of God getting close to God, he takes off!

What are we to do? The answer is as clear as the noonday sun: stop submitting to the devil and start submitting to God! If we will resist the devil, he will flee. If we draw near to God, he will draw near to us! You see, the devil really is something of a coward. When he sees the people of God getting close to God, he takes off!

There is no more urgent and important business for each of us than to draw near to God. If we would be brutally honest with ourselves, we would have to say that we have had our faces towards the devil and our backs towards God. It is time to reverse all of that. It is time to turn our faces towards God and our backs towards the devil.

It is not hard to secure agreement from Christians on this. We quickly and readily agree that we need to draw nearer to the Lord, but are we doing it? Our tendency is to draw near with our lips, but not with our hearts (Matt. 15:8)!

James's next emphasis shows us very plainly and powerfully that drawing near to God is far more than merely mouthing a few words. This emphasis is the second part of his cure for worldliness.

Cleansing our hands and our hearts (v. 8b)

James is calling us to draw near to God by cleaning up both our behaviour ('hands') and our inner lives ('hearts').

Dirty hands and defiled hearts! That's the position that many, many Christians are occupying these days. Their hands are dirty in that they are doing worldly things, things that are out of keeping with God's ownership of their lives. They go to places to which they ought not to go. They say things they ought not to say. They do things they ought not to do. All of these things and more constitute outer behaviour, and all are comprehended and embodied by James's use of the word 'hands'.

But James was not content to call for a change only in the behaviour of his readers. The hands reflect what is in the heart. A. W. Pink observed that the hands and tongues are the shops, and the heart is the warehouse.[2] To call people to cleanse their hands without also calling for them to purify their hearts is pointless.

Why did James think it necessary for his readers to purify their hearts? He said they were 'double-minded', which means they were 'double-souled'. They were not loving God with the whole of their hearts. Their hearts were torn between God and the world.

What does the Bible signify when it uses the word 'heart'? It refers to the totality of the person, that is, to the mind, the will and the affections.

To purify the heart, then, means cleansing the mind, and to cleanse the mind is to rid it of unbiblical thinking. It is to keep out of the mind all those things that are out of keeping with the truth of God as it is revealed in Holy Scripture.

To cleanse the will is to stop making choices that are based on worldly values and to start making our choices and decisions on the basis of the Word of God.

To cleanse the affections is to stop setting our affections—our love—on the temporary, fleeting, frivolous things of this world and to begin setting them on things above (Col. 3:2).

Minds that are informed by the truth of God, choices that are made according to the will of God and affections that are set on the things of God—all will issue into behaviour that is pleasing to God.

That brings us to the third component in James's formula for dealing with worldliness.

Being broken over our sins to the point that we have a truly penitential spirit (vv. 9–10)

Few verses of Scripture are looked upon with less favour than these. This is the day of lightness and frivolity, a day in which we prize laughter so much that we have turned it into an idol. We prize it so much that we regard as good anything that makes us laugh. We confer virtue on anything that brings a chuckle.

Now James is not calling for his readers to be joyless and

miserable. But he is clearly telling them that our sins are not things that we should be laughing about. Gordon Keddie writes, 'When James appeals to world-infected Christians to change their laughter to mourning and their joy to gloom, he is not rejecting Christian joy, but showing them the way to its true enjoyment.'[3] He also writes, 'James wants us to be happy Christians ... but he also wants us to understand that any joy which co-exists with a worldly spirit and practice, and includes the assurance of being right with God, is a dangerous mirage.'[4] Kent Hughes offers this observation: '... while gloom is not a Christian characteristic, mourning over our sin is.'[5]

Why should we mourn over our sins?

Defying God

The first and most obvious answer is because they defy the authority of the God who has made us, the God who has blessed us with innumerable blessings, the God who has given us the supreme blessing of eternal life and the God before whom we must finally stand to give account.

Impeding the work

We must mourn over our sins because they so grievously impede the work of the Lord. The sins of Christians cause unbelievers to think that Christians are no different from themselves and, therefore, that the gospel is nothing in which they should be interested.

Depriving us of joy

We must mourn over our sins because they rob us of true

joy. The devil, ever the liar, tells us that keeping God's laws brings misery, and breaking them brings happiness. But the long history of mankind shows us again and again that sinful living destroys and wrecks. It can destroy our health. It can destroy our homes. It can destroy our churches. It can even destroy life.

Where is the joy in all of that? Yes, sin brings pleasure for a season, but the season is always short and the consequences are always great.

We have looked, then, at James's prescription for getting back to where we as Christians should be. It is not an easy road, but it is a tried and true road. It is the road of submission, cleansing and brokenness.

Christians often wonder why we do not see true spiritual awakening. Could it be that the awakening we need waits at the door? It waits for us to follow the formula that James has laid out for us.

FOR FURTHER STUDY

1. Read John 8:44; 1 Peter 5:8; Revelation 12:9. What names do these verses use for Satan?

2. Read Ephesians 6:10–20. What strategy does Paul give for fighting Satan?

TO THINK ABOUT AND DISCUSS

1. What can you do to cleanse your mind, will and affections?

2. What does the word 'repent' mean to you?

18 When nobodies act like somebodies

(4:11–17)

Pride is a funny thing. We can easily spot it in others, but we can't see it in ourselves. Some of the proudest people I have ever met thought of themselves as being very humble and were very critical of pride in others. Most of us are a lot prouder than we would like to believe.

P ride is not a new thing. It began even before this world was created. The first swelling of pride was in the heart of Lucifer (Isa. 14:12–14). It led to him being cast out of heaven and becoming Satan, the adversary of God and of the people of God. From that sad beginning so long ago, pride has roared through human history. It has never gone out of existence.

James could see it in his readers. He wrote the words of our text in order to warn them about two manifestations of it.

The first was …

Speaking evil of one another (vv. 11–12)

Curtis Vaughan writes, 'To "speak evil" … of a person is to find fault with him, to speak disparagingly of him, to gossip maliciously about him.'[1] Some people think fault-finding is their spiritual gift!

How sad this is! They were brothers and sisters in Jesus Christ. They were members of the same body. And they were turning on one another. It was like the body attacking itself! Suppose my hands started attacking my feet, bringing blood and inflicting severe pain. What a strange sight that would be! But it is no more strange than that which is going on in many churches!

Christians attacking one another! We have a tendency to dismiss it as a trivial thing. James refuses to do so. He wants his readers to stare this ugly thing in the face. He begins by telling them that such evil-speaking means setting themselves above the law.

There is a law against evil-speaking. It is God's law. When we carve up a brother or sister in Christ, we are breaking that law. But we are doing more. We are suggesting that we know better than God who gave the law. We are saying that this law should not even be a law. Curtis Vaughan observes, 'The man who deliberately breaks a law thereby disparages that law. In effect he sets himself above it and declares that it is a bad law, not worthy to be obeyed.'[2]

Think of it in these terms: if I speed through a construction zone, I am essentially saying that the people in authority, who set the speed limit, did not know what they were doing. I know better than those people and their law! I am, therefore, putting myself above the law. Gordon Keddie notes, 'Law works that way: you either submit to it or set yourself above it!'[3]

When we break one of God's laws, then, we are setting ourselves above God. Now that is pride! And that is begging for trouble! When we set ourselves up against God, we forget that he is the one who has the power both to save and to destroy (v. 12).

Be sure of this: God is not going to let us get away with thumbing our noses at him and his laws. Curtis Vaughan says of God, 'He may delegate various functions and responsibilities to human representatives, but He permits no man to share His judgment seat, or to cancel or modify His laws.'[4]

Yes, thank God, he has the power to save! Where would we be without that? But he also has the power to destroy! We tend to forget that, but it is just as true as the saving part.

> How many of God's blessings have we forfeited because we spoke evil?

James is saying that evil-speaking always has a price tag attached, and it is a heavy price! Before we buy the product, we should look at the tag. Before we engage in evil-speaking, we should remember that the God who can destroy has promised to judge such speaking. That judgement takes place to a certain extent in this life. How many of God's blessings have we forfeited because we spoke evil? How many friendships have been ruined? How many people have been driven from the church? How many church leaders have been driven into discouragement? How many of their children have been driven into disillusionment? Is this a price we are willing to pay in order to enjoy the delicious feeling of cutting up a brother or sister in Christ?

If God's judgement doesn't find us here, it will find us in eternity. But it will find us! Make no mistake about that!

Perhaps the thing that we most need to carry away from James's message is this question: 'Who are you to judge another?' (v. 12). We might put it in these words: 'Who do you think you are?' This is what God asks each of us when we engage in verbally shredding our brothers and sisters in Christ—'Who do you think you are?'

The second manifestation of pride that James could see among his readers was …

Planning without regard to God (vv. 13–17)

James could see his readers doing exactly that. They would talk about going to 'such and such a city', about spending a year or so there and about the various transactions they would conduct while they were there (v. 13). They were talking as if they were in charge of their lives, and they weren't.

James tells them that they had not factored into the equation the brevity and unpredictability of life. They could talk about one place, that city over there, and, before they could get there, end up in another place—eternity. They could talk about a period of time, this year or next, and, before that period began, find themselves in the realm of the timeless.

How easily we forget what life is like! It is a vapour! It is like the morning mist that lingers only in the early morning hours and vanishes when the sun rises. And when the sun rises, it doesn't take long for the vapour to vanish!

So James tells his readers to quit acting as if they are in control. That is proud living! He says, 'Instead you ought to say, "If the Lord wills, we shall live and do this or that"' (v. 15).

No, he is not suggesting that we actually have to say those exact words every single time we are planning to go somewhere or to transact some business—although it would not be a bad idea to say them frequently! Rather he is talking about always keeping in mind that God is in control, and none of our plans ever supersedes or overrides his plans.

The eternal God has made us for eternity, and to eternity we must go. And the eternity that awaits us is one either of bliss or of woe!

So let us live with God and eternity weighing much on our minds. We constantly have the tendency to make this life the main event and eternity a footnote. Eternity is the main event, and only a fool lives as if this life is all that there is.

Don't count on your time. It is passing! Don't count on your possessions. They will soon belong to someone else. Don't count on your career. It will soon be over. But count on this: eternity is rapidly approaching, and only those who have taken refuge in Jesus Christ can face it.

FOR FURTHER STUDY

1. Read Psalm 39:4–6. What do these verses teach about life in this world?
2. Read 1 Peter 2:1–3. What does Peter tell us to put away and to desire?

TO THINK ABOUT AND DISCUSS

1. List some results you have noticed from Christians engaging in evil speaking.
2. How can you avoid planning without regard to God?

19 Misused money

(5:1–6)

The Bible is not against us having riches. It is against us misusing our riches.

J ames could see among his readers the tendency to have an undue interest in and preoccupation with wealth. He could have just turned his head, but he cared too much for them and their welfare. So he sounded a warning, and it is a stern warning indeed.

We can divide his words into two parts. First, he speaks of …

The heavy price tag attached to misused wealth (vv. 1–3)

Misuse leads to miseries! James could see those miseries coming towards his readers, and he assures them that those miseries are of such a nature that they should even now begin to weep and howl (v. 1).

James leaves no doubt about the nature of these miseries. He sets them in the clear light of day.

In the here and now (vv. 2–3a)

The first is the misery of seeing our riches rot.

Wealth in those days consisted of three things: grain, clothing and precious metals. Not one of these things lasts! Some think that James had grain in mind when he used the word 'riches' in verse 2. If so, his point is that grain eventually rots. And fine clothes are not immune from ruin, but are eaten by moths (v. 2). And precious metals are 'corroded'. No, James was not suggesting that gold and silver could actually rust. This was probably his way of saying that they drop in value.

James's point is not hard to grasp. If we are obsessed with grain, clothes and precious metals, we cannot help but weep and howl when they are gone.

In the hereafter (v. 3)

The second misery of misused wealth will be found in the hereafter. James says it will 'eat your flesh like fire'.

Misused wealth will cause pain in the future. Those who make riches the primary thing in this life and live without regard to God will be keenly aware of their folly. Their memory of living for wealth when they could have lived for God will bite and burn like fire!

Then they will realize that they 'heaped up treasure in the last days' (v. 3). In eternity, they will see that they accumulated wealth as if they would live for ever, but all the while they were living the last days of their lives. They were speeding towards eternity while they were amassing their riches.

We surely cannot read James's words without thinking

of Jesus's parable of the rich fool (Luke 12:13–21). A farmer raised such a huge crop that he did not have enough room to store the harvest. He decided to pull down his old barns and build larger ones. Finally, the project was complete. The larger barns had been built, and the crop had been stored in the barns. The man thought he had it made, saying to himself, '… you have many goods laid up for many years; take your ease; eat, drink, and be merry' (Luke 12:19).

But while he was racing around to accumulate his wealth, death was racing towards him! God said to him, 'Fool! This night your soul will be required of you; then whose will those things be which you have provided?' (Luke 12:20).

In wrapping up the story, Jesus left no room for doubt about its meaning: 'So is he who lays up treasure for himself, and is not rich toward God' (Luke 12:21).

There is, then, a heavy price tag indeed attached to misused wealth. Having established that, James proceeds to his second emphasis.

Some manifestations of misused wealth (vv. 3–6)

The first of these is …

Hoarding (v. 3)

James warns his readers that they have 'heaped up treasure'.

Scripture never tells us that we should not save money. It urges us to be wise, and it is wise to give thought to the future and to plan prudently for it.

Hoarding takes place when we continue to accumulate above and beyond that which is necessary. We have all heard stories about elderly people living in foul conditions while subsisting on dog food or cat food. They were assumed to be very poor, but were discovered to have great wealth when they passed away. Such people are examples of hoarders.

The second of these manifestations is …

Depriving workers of their rightful wages (v. 4)

The Old Testament consistently condemns fraudulent treatment of workers (Lev. 19:13; Deut. 24:14–15; Prov. 3:27–28). But some were ignoring those commands.

The rich would certainly not have been hurt by paying the wages. They had plenty from which to pay! But the workers, who lived from day to day and from hand to mouth, were hurt tremendously by not getting paid.

James depicts the seriousness of the matter in terms of two cries going up to God. The first is the cry of the unpaid wages. James pictures them sitting there in the bank and crying out to God because they have not been sent to those to whom they should have gone.

The second is the cry of the workers themselves. It is the cry of anguish, as they sit down with their families to eat a crust of bread or nothing at all when they could have been eating a decent meal.

These cries do not go unnoticed. They are heard by 'the Lord of Sabaoth' (v. 4). The Bible uses many names for God. He is such a glorious being that no one name

> The God who is greater than all the hosts of heaven is certainly great enough to mete out justice to the cruel fat cats who inflict such pain and misery on their workers!

can do justice to him. The name James uses here means 'Lord of hosts'. It tells us that God is surrounded by hosts of angelic beings, and that he is greater than all of them. He is their Lord.

The God who is greater than all the hosts of heaven is certainly great enough to mete out justice to the cruel fat cats who inflict such pain and misery on their workers!

The third misuse of wealth is ...

Wallowing in luxury and self-indulgence (v. 5)

Here James is talking about people who use their wealth to pamper themselves. Needs are on every hand, needs that could be easily alleviated by some generosity. But these people are oblivious to the needs. Thinking only of themselves and their comfort, they go on buying and buying.

James has a devastating word for all such. They are fattening themselves for God's judgement. As a calf eats and eats without realizing that it is fattening itself for the day of slaughter, so the pampered gorge themselves without realizing that there is 'a day of slaughter' coming (v. 5).

A final misuse James mentions is ...

Murdering the innocent (v. 6)

We are not to picture any of James's readers going out with swords to hack people to death. James has something far more subtle in mind—but just as deadly! Kent Hughes explains: 'James is referring to judicial "murder"—primarily referring to taking away the means of making a living. The landed gentry controlled the courts. The poor could not oppose them because they had no way to use the system, and thus were helpless.'[1] There is more than one way to murder!

James's words about murdering the just who are not able to resist (v. 6) make us think about the Lord Jesus Christ. Although he was just in every way, he was murdered. And although he certainly had the power to resist, he did not do so. He willingly submitted to unjust treatment so he could provide eternal salvation for sinners.

All sinners are urged to come to Christ. The rich are urged to become poor, recognizing that their riches cannot save them. They are told to come to Christ, saying,

> Nothing in my hand I bring,
> Simply to Thy cross I cling.
>
> (Augustus M. Toplady)

And the poor are given the assurance that there are riches in Christ Jesus that this world can never offer.

But all must come to Christ! And all who come to Christ will be truly changed, and that change will show up in how they use their money.

For further study ▶

FOR FURTHER STUDY

1. Read Matthew 6:19–21. What does Jesus say about our priorities?
2. Read Psalm 62:10. What does this verse caution us about?

TO THINK ABOUT AND DISCUSS

1. What are some of the indications that people have become obsessed with material things that you can see in the world around us? in the church?
2. Why is it wrong to focus on wealth?

20 Some good reasons for a good thing

(5:7–12)

There can be no doubt that James had the need for patience on his mind when he wrote these words. Four times he uses some form of the word 'patience' (vv. 7–8, 10). He also uses the words 'endure' and 'perseverance' (v. 11).

James knew that his readers needed two kinds of patience. As we have noted frequently, these people were facing persecution because of their faith. Therefore, they needed that kind of patience that enabled them to put up with their hardships without retaliating. They needed patience in their suffering.

They also needed the kind of patience that would enable them lovingly to endure trying and exasperating conduct on the part of their fellow-believers. This is the reason James tells them not to 'grumble' against one another (v. 9).

We need the same kinds of patience. When trials and difficulties come our way, it is very easy for us to question

God, to doubt his goodness and to complain about his dealings with us.

And we always need patience in our dealings with one another. We are all very flawed, and we can very easily vex our brothers and sisters in Christ. We need to realize when we do so that we are not giving a good witness to those around us.

James was not content merely to call for patience. He also gave his readers some powerful incentives for seeking it.

The first reason is …

The common bond they shared in Christ (vv. 7, 9–10, 12)

It is not incidental or accidental that James calls them 'brethren' four times in these verses.

This has particular reference to the need to be patient with one another. When we are inclined to be critical and grumpy about a brother in Christ, we would do well to remember that he is our brother in Christ! And what we share in Christ is far greater than anything which may tend to divide us. Our need, then, is to focus on the major thing that unites us rather than the minor thing that divides us.

The second reason is …

The coming of the Lord Jesus Christ (vv. 7–9)

James twice mentions the 'coming of the Lord'. He also says, '… the Judge is standing at the door.'

His words have led to considerable debate. Did James expect the Lord Jesus Christ to come during his lifetime? If he did, he was mistaken. How are we to square that mistake with his authority as an apostle?

I suggest that James is here reflecting the very thing that the Lord Jesus himself taught: 'Watch therefore, for you do not know what hour your Lord is coming' (Matt. 24:42).

Every generation of Christians has been called to live with the awareness that the Lord could come at any time, and to let that awareness shape their lives.

When it comes to the matter of responsibility, we should act as if the Lord's coming is far away. In other words, we should not be sitting in idleness because we are expecting him to return. We are to be up and doing. We are to be planning and carrying out our plans.

But when it comes to the matter of accountability, remembering that we must answer for all we do and all we fail to do, we must act as if the Lord is coming today. We would grumble less if we thought about judgement more!

The third incentive James gives for patience is this ...

The good example set by others (vv. 7, 10–11)

James gives three examples in these verses.

The farmer (v. 7).

The farmers of those days were dependent on two 'rains'. The 'early' rain came at planting time in October. The 'latter' rain came at harvesting time in late April or early May. Without those two rains, the farmer had no hope of raising a good crop.

But the farmer could not force it to rain. All he could do was wait for the rains to come. He had to depend on the God who had ordained those rains to send them at the proper time.

We don't have to share the growing season of James to learn the lesson he was driving home. We are called to trust God in circumstances over which we have no control.

The prophets (v. 10)

These men are well known for suffering wrong when they had done no wrong. They were harshly treated for faithfully declaring the word of God.

How these men suffered! For over forty years, Moses had to endure a complaining and grumbling people. Jeremiah, the weeping prophet, was thrown into the mud of an empty cistern. Daniel was cast into a lions' den. Zechariah, the son of Jehoiada, sealed his testimony with his blood, as he was put to death in the temple (2 Chr. 24:20–22).

James alluded to such prophets to urge his readers to be patient when they themselves were suffering for doing good.

Job (v. 11)

We know Job's story very well. He was very devoted and faithful to the Lord, and he was very prosperous and happy. And then the devil came along and suggested that Job was faithful because he was blessed. If his blessings were removed, his devotion to God would vanish!

So the Lord allowed Satan to test Job, and test he did! Job lost his family, his health and his possessions. But in the end, Job still had his faith, and the devil was proven wrong.

In citing the example of Job, James refers to 'the end intended by the Lord'. And that end was to show 'that the Lord is very compassionate and merciful' (v. 11).

By reminding his readers of Job, James was calling them

to trust God to have a good purpose even in the midst of circumstances that they did not understand.

We are called to this same kind of patience, but, oh, how difficult it is for us! We look at this harsh circumstance and that unpleasant reality, and we are very ready and eager to pronounce an adverse verdict on God. If the Lord truly had our best interests at heart, he would not allow such things! These difficulties are so great that there could not possibly be a good purpose behind them!

If we will let him, the devil will always have us drawing false conclusions about God on the basis of our burdens and trials.

What are we to do? We must learn how to talk to the devil! And when he suggests that our circumstances are such that they could not conceivably come from the hand of a good God, we must learn to point him to the cross of Calvary. That is where God for ever declared how he feels about his children. He put his only Son there to bear the wrath of God in their stead.

> If we will let him, the devil will always have us drawing false conclusions about God on the basis of our burdens and trials.

As we point Satan to the cross, we must say to him, 'God did so much for me there that I can never question his love for me. God did so much for me there that if he chooses to do nothing else for me at all, I will still have cause to praise him forever.'

The cross is ever the great antidote for whatever ails the

> The cross is ever the great antidote for whatever ails the Christian.

Christian. And if we will learn to always take the devil and his insinuations there, he will leave us and take his insinuations with him!

We have examined in brief fashion the plea that James made to his readers for patience. We must not leave his words without noticing one more thing, namely, their enemy in achieving patience. He says to them, 'Establish your hearts …' (v. 8). Alec Motyer puts it neatly: 'Whatever our life-style, the heart lies at the centre.'[1]

If we are failing in patiently trusting the Lord, it is because we have not fixed our hearts with determination and resolve. So let us give attention to our hearts. That is where the battle rages, and that is where the battle is lost or won.

Let us talk to God about our hearts. Let's tell him how prone our hearts are to take us away from God. And let's fill our hearts with the truth of the Word of God. If we are to live for God, we must all be good heart doctors.

FOR FURTHER STUDY

1. Read 1 Peter 2:18–25. What example does Peter give of patience? How did this person express patience?

2. Read 1 Thessalonians 4:13–18. What does Paul teach about the coming of the Lord?

TO THINK ABOUT AND DISCUSS

1. What can you do to increase your awareness of Christ's coming? What difference should this increased awareness make to your life?

2. What can you do to 'doctor' your heart so you can trust the Lord more?

21 What to do with ...

(5:13–18)

We are living in a 'What to do with ...' society. We pick up a magazine, and we are told what to do with this situation or that. We go to the Internet, and we are told what to do with first one problem and then another.

This is the 'list' generation. We love lists: ten steps to this, five keys to that, seven principles for something else. We like lists because they are so practical!

The Bible was dealing with practical matters long before we ever came along, and, unless the Lord Jesus soon returns, it will continue to do so after we are gone. For centuries and centuries, the Bible has been telling us what to do with various situations.

And while all of the Bible is practical, no part of it is more so than the book of James. In the verses before us, James gives us a list of what we should do with various situations. He begins with ...

Life in general (v. 13)

Life consists of two parts: the bad and the good. Alec Motyer writes,

> Here, then, in two words, are all life's experiences, and each of them in turn can so easily be the occasion of spiritual upset. Trouble can give rise to an attitude of surly rebellion against God and the abandonment of spiritual practices. Equally, times of ease and affluence beget complacency, laziness and the assumption that we are able of ourselves to cope with life, and God is forgotten. [1]

James has a word for us no matter what life brings our way. When things are bad, he tells us to pray. When things are good, he tells us to praise.

We can put it like this: Christians should find themselves naturally gravitating towards God in every situation of life.

With that in place, James turns to ...

A special challenge that life often puts before us (vv. 14–15)

This is the challenge of sickness. We can consider James's teaching on this matter under three sub-headings.

A specific request

When a believer contracts an illness, he or she must take the initiative and contact the elders of the church.

We should note that James is not talking here about a case of the sniffles. According to Curtis Vaughan, the Greek word translated 'sick' refers to a sickness that incapacitates a person for work. The Puritan Thomas Manton says, 'The elders must not be sent for upon every light occasion, as soon as the head or foot acheth … but in such grievous diseases wherein there is danger and great pain.'[2]

We should also note that the elders are those who exercise pastoral oversight and spiritual leadership within the church. Many churches tend to invest these things in one man, but the New Testament ideal is a plurality of elders (Acts 11:30; 14:23; 15:4, 6; 20:17; 21:18; Titus 1:5).

A twofold response

The elders are to respond to the request of the sick person in two ways. First, they are to pray. Second, they are to anoint the sick person with oil.

We understand the importance of prayer. Healing comes only from God. So we must go to the source of it if we would have it.

The anointing with oil is the part that creates controversy. Are we to take this oil to be medicinal in nature? The good Samaritan, we recall, treated the wounded man with oil and wine—the former to sooth and the latter to cleanse (Luke 10:34).[3] If this is the correct understanding, James was telling sick people to ask for prayer and go to the doctor.

Or are we, as some suggest, to understand the oil as a symbol or emblem of divine grace? If this is correct, James was telling the sick to ask for prayer and to trust the Lord.

It is probably safe to say, as Alec Motyer does, that the sick and the elders would have both the spiritual and the medicinal in mind as they went through this process.[4]

A twofold promise

Having laid out the procedure to be followed, James promises healing for the sick and forgiveness for sin.

We can dispose of the latter without too much difficulty. James was not saying that each and every sickness we experience is due to some sort of sin. But he was saying that some sickness has sin as its root. In such a case, the Lord will give the sick person the awareness that this is the case, along with forgiveness for the sin.

The promise of healing as a result of 'the prayer of faith' is much more complex. The promise seems to be a blanket guarantee that healing will be granted each time the process is followed.

The problem, of course, concerns those many times when the process has been followed, and there has been no healing. When such instances occur, the usual explanation is that we have failed to have faith. We assume that faith is ours to work up and that we should be able to do so at any moment. If healing does not come, it is our fault. We haven't worked up the faith.

> '... the prayer of faith is not something we can manufacture by saying "I believe, I believe, I believe, I really believe, I truly believe, I double believe!" *It is a gift from God'*.

But the Bible says faith is a gift of God (Eph. 2:8). When it is his will to heal, the Lord grants the persuasion that he will grant the healing and enables the elders to pray 'the prayer of faith'. Kent

Hughes explains: '... the prayer of faith is not something we can manufacture by saying "I believe, I believe, I believe, I really believe, I truly believe, I double believe!" *It is a gift from God*' (italics are his).[5] Hughes then shares these words from John Blanchard: 'The "prayer offered in faith" is circular in shape; it begins and ends in heaven, in the sovereign will of God.'[6]

It comes down to this: the sick person is to call for the elders, the elders are to anoint and pray, and God will do as he pleases.

James also tells us ...

What to do with sin (vv. 16–18)

His words remind us that people who truly know the Lord Jesus Christ still sin. We will not be completely freed from it until we leave this world and enter into eternal glory.

Sometimes we sin against one another. What are we to do in such situations? James tells us to confess such sins and to pray for one another (v. 16).

Confession should always be as wide as the sin. If we have sinned secretly, we should confess it to God. If we have sinned against someone else, we should confess it to God and to the person whom we have wronged. And if we have sinned publicly, we should confess it to God and in public.

Furthermore, if a fellow-believer comes to us to confess that he or she has sinned against us, we must always be willing to grant forgiveness. Only in this way can we be 'healed' or reconciled.

We cannot leave this portion of James's letter without noting the profound emphasis he puts on prayer. Prayer has been a strong emphasis throughout this letter. It is not surprising, then, that James would mention it again towards the end. In this case, James asserts that 'The effective, fervent prayer of a righteous man avails much' (v. 16).

Do we doubt this assertion? James has the answer for us. He urges us to consider the example of the prophet Elijah. There can be no doubt that Elijah's praying accomplished much. He prayed, and there was no rain; and he prayed again, and there was rain. But the key thing is that he prayed! And that is the key thing for us! Are we praying?

We have a tendency to dismiss the example of Elijah and the examples of others who were mighty in prayer. We think they were super-saints, and prayer was in some way different for them.

But James reminds us that Elijah was made out of the same stuff as all the rest of us (v. 17). The secret to his praying was not that he was a superman. The secret was that he prayed!

And James's point is plain. No matter what life brings our way, let's make sure we do not forget to pray. And let's make sure that our praying is not merely mouthing words, but an earnest seeking after God. Only then do we truly pray, and only then do we experience our own great things.

For further study ▶

FOR FURTHER STUDY

1. Read 1 John 1:8–10. What do these verses teach about sin and confession?
2. Read 2 Timothy 4:20. What does Paul's statement about Trophimus tell us about sickness and healing?

TO THINK ABOUT AND DISCUSS

1. How can you use sickness to glorify God?
2. What is your response to the section on confessing sin? If there is someone to whom you need to confess, go to that person without delay.

22 Winning the wanderer

(5:19–20)

We have found throughout our studies in James that it is a very practical book. That continues to the very end. In his closing verses, James urges his readers to take up a wonderful work.

The problem which James addresses (v. 19)

James writes, 'Brethren, if anyone among you wanders from the truth …'

He is quite obviously writing to believers in Christ. He has often addressed his fellow-believers as his 'brethren', and he does so again here.

'Brethren' is one of the most prized words in the Christian vocabulary. It reminds us of great privileges. Christians have been freed from servitude to Satan and placed into the family of God. Therefore, they have God as their Father, and they are brothers and sisters in Christ.

But even though they enjoy great spiritual privileges, Christian people are capable of wandering or straying. They can and do backslide.

Backsliders do not lose their salvation. How thankful we should be for that! Backsliding means wandering from the truth (v. 19).

What is it to wander from the truth? It means loosening our grip on the Word of God to the point that we do not hold as firmly as we once did to its teachings. And that always leads to the loosening of the Bible's grip on how we live.

James's description of the backslider should make all of us heed the words of Proverbs 23:23: 'Buy the truth, and do not sell it …'

The action James proposes (vv. 19–20)

Believers have a responsibility to fellow-believers who stray. What is the nature of that responsibility? James says it is to turn them back (v. 19). It is to turn the sinner 'from the error of his way' (v. 20).

> Believers have a responsibility to fellow-believers who stray.

The word 'turn' is translated 'convert' in some versions. This terminology has caused some to believe that this passage deals with winning the lost instead of reclaiming the backslidden. But the Lord Jesus himself used the word 'convert' in reference to a backslidden saint. Jesus said to Simon Peter, '… when thou are converted, strengthen thy brethren' (Luke 22:32, KJV).

Simon was about to enter a period of terrible backsliding. He would deny the Lord Jesus three times in the space of a few hours. But he would be 'converted' from his backsliding. He would be turned from it.

Gordon Keddie says the term 'conversion' can apply

to 'any significant turning-point in our spiritual lives …'[1] He also writes, 'The Christian life may be punctuated by a number of such episodes of wandering away from truth and "conversion" again back to Christ's "straight and narrow way".'[2]

We can say, therefore, that backslidden Christians need a conversion. They need to be turned back to the Lord. And James urges their fellow-Christians to get in their way, head them off and turn them back.

Many of us must admit that we have not thought much about this. When we see a Christian straying, we have a tendency to excuse ourselves from responsibility by saying, 'It's not my business.'

Or we think that our responsibility begins and ends with praying for the backslidden. James would certainly have us to pray for them. But he wants us also to confront them lovingly with their straying and tenderly call them back to the Lord.

We have noticed that the Lord Jesus predicted the denials of Simon Peter. Those denials took place in sickening fashion! And with each denial, Simon strayed farther from the Lord until he was very far away indeed. But the Lord Jesus did not leave Simon Peter in his backslidden condition. He pursued him and restored him (John 21).

The Lord Jesus is our example in this area, as he is in every other area. So let us not stand idly by when we see a straying brother or sister!

The assurance James offers (v. 20)

James could not be content only to call his readers to the work of reclaiming the wanderer. He also provides the incentive for doing so. The Christian who reclaims a backslider accomplishes great things indeed.

The Christian will turn a sinner 'from the error of his way'

If backsliding is turning from the truth, to reclaim the backslider is to turn him or her back towards the truth.

The Christian will 'save a soul from death'

What did James mean by this? He may have been thinking about the Lord ending the life of the backslider as a punishment for his or her sin. We do not like to hear it, but there is such a thing as sin that leads to death (1 John 5:16–17)!

When we go about the business of reclaiming a backslider, we do not always know what we are achieving. We may be saving that person from an early grave!

Or James might have had something else in mind. He might have been suggesting that a backslidden condition is like a spiritual deadness in the heart. In this case, the one who reclaims a backslider is rescuing him or her from that deadness.

Whatever James had in mind, it is apparent that backsliding is a very serious thing indeed. It is also apparent that anyone who helps the backslider is doing a wonderful thing.

The Christian will 'cover a multitude of sins'

Gordon Keddie suggests that the word 'cover' takes us back to the ark of the covenant and the mercy seat of the Old Testament.[3]

The ark was a box in which the Law of Moses was placed. Above the box were stationed cherubim, who represented God himself. If the ark consisted of nothing more, it would have done nothing but give testimony to an awesome reality, namely, God taking note of our disobedience to his holy law.

But there was another part of the ark. Thank God it was there! The mercy seat! The mercy seat was a flat gold plate that sat between the box and the cherubim. When the high priest of Israel made atonement for the sins of the people, he would take the blood of a sacrifice and sprinkle it on the mercy seat. And the blood of the mercy seat covered the broken law! It was as if God could not see the sin because of the blood!

All of this was designed, of course, to picture the redeeming work of the Lord Jesus. The blood that he shed on the cross covers the sins of all those who believe in him.

But that same blood also covers the sins of Christians who backslide. Keddie says, '… it is this rich theology of covering which is associated with the winning of others to Christ, for the obvious reason that it is the same blood-bought salvation which alike saves the pagan and the backslidden Christian.'[4]

We end our study, then, on the highest of all notes—the glorious work of Jesus. But we must not leave James without thinking again about some of the key points which we have studied. Warren Wiersbe summarizes those points by urging each Christian to ask him- or herself a series of probing questions:

1. Am I becoming more and more patient in the testings of life?
2. Do I play with temptation or resist it from the start?
3. Do I find joy in obeying the Word of God, or do I merely study it and learn it?
4. Are there any prejudices that shackle me?
5. Am I able to control my tongue?
6. Am I a peacemaker rather than a troublemaker? Do people come to me for spiritual wisdom?
7. Am I a friend of God or a friend of the world?
8. Do I make plans without considering the will of God?
9. Am I selfish when it comes to money? Am I unfaithful in the paying of my bills?
10. Do I naturally depend on prayer when I find myself in some kind of trouble?
11. Am I the kind of person others seek for prayer support?
12. What is my attitude toward the wandering brother? Do I criticize and gossip, or do I seek to restore him in love?

Having posed these questions, Wiersbe winds up his commentary with this exhortation: 'Don't just grow old—grow up!'[5]

May God himself help us to do so!

FOR FURTHER STUDY

1. Read Proverbs 14:14. What does this verse teach about backsliding?
2. Read Hosea 14:1–4. What do these verses tell us to do about backsliding? What do they promise?

TO THINK ABOUT AND DISCUSS

1. What can you do to tighten your grip on the Word of God?
2. Do you know a believer who has backslidden? What can you do to help this person get back to where he or she needs to be?

Endnotes

Overview

1 Quoted in Simon J. Kistemaker, *Exposition of the Epistle of James and the Epistles of John* (New Testament Commentary; Grand Rapids, MI: Baker, 1986), p. 10.

Chapter 2

1 Cited by Gordon Keddie, *The Practical Christian* (Darlington: Evangelical Press, 1989), p. 35.

Chapter 3

1 Cited by R. Kent Hughes, *James: Faith That Works* (Wheaton, IL: Crossway, 1991), p. 35.
2 Ibid.
3 Ibid., p. 36.

Chapter 4

1 Ibid., p. 46.
2 Ibid.
3 Curtis Vaughan, *A Study Guide: James* (Grand Rapids, MI: Zondervan, 1969), p. 31.
4 Cited by Vaughan, *James*, p. 31.
5 Ibid.
6 Ibid.
7 Hughes, *James*, p. 49.
8 Keddie, *The Practical Christian*, p. 53.

Chapter 5

1 Hughes, *James*, p. 53.
2 Ibid., p. 55.
3 Matthew Henry, *Matthew Henry's Commentary*, vol. vi (Tappan, NJ: Fleming H. Revell [n.d.]), p. 972.
4 Hughes, *James*, p. 57.
5 Vaughan, *James*, p. 33.
6 Cited by Vaughan, *James*, p. 33.

Chapter 6

1 Cited by Hughes, *James*, p. 64.
2 Cited by Vaughan, *James*, p. 37.
3 Ibid., p. 38.

Chapter 7

1 From Hughes, *James*, p. 73.

2 Vaughan, *James*, p. 40.

3 Ibid.

4 Cited by Vaughan, *James*, p. 40.

Chapter 8

1 Hughes, *James*, p. 80.

2 Ibid., pp. 81–82.

Chapter 9

1 From Keddie, *The Practical Christian*, p. 93.

Chapter 10

1 Ibid., p. 102.

2 Vaughan, *James*, p.53.

3 Hughes, *James*, p. 102.

4 Vaughan, *James*, p. 54.

Chapter 11

1 Hughes, p. 108.

2 Cited by Warren W. Wiersbe, *The Bible Exposition Commentary*, vol. ii (Wheaton, IL: Victor Books, 1989), p. 354.

3 Hughes, *James*, p. 111.

4 Ibid.

5 Keddie, *The Practical Christian*, pp. 113–114.

Chapter 12

1 Vaughan, *James*, p. 63.

2 Cited by Hughes, *James*, p. 122.

Chapter 13

1 Ibid., p. 126.

Chapter 14

1 Ibid., p. 139.

2 Ibid., p. 141.

Chapter 15

1 Charles R. Erdman, *An Exposition: The General Epistles* (Philadelphia: The Westminster Press, 1919), p. 32.

Chapter 17

1 Keddie, *The Practical Christian*, p. 163.

2 A. W. Pink, *The Doctrine of Salvation* (Grand Rapids, MI: Baker, 1975), p. 155.

3 Keddie, *The Practical Christian*, p. 163.

4 Ibid.

5 Hughes, *James*, p. 189.

Chapter 18

1 Vaughan, *James*, p. 93.
2 Ibid.
3 Keddie, *The Practical Christian*, p. 171.
4 Vaughan, *James*, p. 94.

Chapter 19

1 Hughes, *James*, p. 218.

Chapter 20

1 Alec Motyer, *The Message of James* (Leicester: Inter-Varsity Press, 1985), p. 181.

Chapter 21

1 Ibid., p. 187.
2 Cited by Vaughan, *James*, p. 116.
3 Motyer, *The Message of James*, p. 192.
4 Ibid., p. 195.
5 Hughes, *James*, p. 258.
6 Ibid.

Chapter 22

1 Keddie, *The Practical Christian*, p. 224.
2 Ibid.
3 Ibid., p. 225.

4 Ibid.
5 Wiersbe, *Bible Exposition Commentary*, p. 385.

Opening up series

Title	Author	ISBN
Opening up 1 Corinthians	Derek Prime	978–1–84625–004–0
Opening up 1 Thessalonians	Tim Shenton	978–1–84625–031–6
Opening up 1 Timothy	Simon J Robinson	978–1–903087–69–5
Opening up 2 & 3 John	Terence Peter Crosby	978–1–84625–023–1
Opening up 2 Peter	Clive Anderson	978–1–84625–077–4
Opening up 2 Thessalonians	Ian McNaughton	978–1–84625–117–7
Opening up 2 Timothy	Peter Williams	978–1–84625–065–1
Opening up Amos	Michael Bentley	978–1–84625–041–5
Opening up Colossians & Philemon	Ian McNaughton	978–1–84625–016–3
Opening up Ecclesiastes	Jim Winter	978–1–903087–86–2
Opening up Exodus	Iain D Campbell	978–1–84625–029–3
Opening up Ezekiel's visions	Peter Jeffery	978–1–903087–66–4
Opening up Ezra	Peter Williams	978–1–84625–022–4
Opening up Haggai	Peter Williams	978–1–84625–144–3
Opening up Hebrews	Philip Hacking	978–1–84625–042–2
Opening up Jonah	Paul Mackrell	978–1–84625–080–4
Opening up Joshua	Roger Ellsworth	978–1–84625–118–4
Opening up Judges	Simon J Robinson	978–1–84625–043–9
Opening up Luke's Gospel	Gavin Childress	978–1–84625–030–9
Opening up Malachi	Roger Ellsworth	978–1–84625–033–0
Opening up Matthew	Iain D Campbell	978–1–84625–116–0
Opening up Nahum	Clive Anderson	978–1–903087–74–9
Opening up Philippians	Roger Ellsworth	978–1–903087–64–0
Opening up Proverbs	Jim Newheiser	978–1–84625–110–8
Opening up Psalms	Roger Ellsworth	978–1–84625–005–7
Opening up Ruth	Jonathan Prime	978–1–84625–067–5
Opening up Titus	David Campbell	978–1–84625–079–8
Opening up Zephaniah	Michael Bentley	978–1–84625–111–5

About Day One:

Day One's threefold commitment:

- To be faithful to the Bible, God's inerrant, infallible Word;
- To be relevant to our modern generation;
- To be excellent in our publication standards.

I continue to be thankful for the publications of Day One. They are biblical; they have sound theology; and they are relative to the issues at hand. The material is condensed and manageable while, at the same time, being complete—a challenging balance to find. We are happy in our ministry to make use of these excellent publications.

JOHN MACARTHUR, PASTOR-TEACHER, GRACE COMMUNITY CHURCH, CALIFORNIA

It is a great encouragement to see Day One making such excellent progress. Their publications are always biblical, accessible and attractively produced, with no compromise on quality. Long may their progress continue and increase!

JOHN BLANCHARD, AUTHOR, EVANGELIST AND APOLOGIST

Visit our websites for more information and to request a free catalogue of our books.

UK:
www.dayone.co.uk

North America:
www.dayonebookstore.com